WOMEN OF PEACE
FINDING LOVE & PEACE WITHIN

Visionary Author, Latoya Jackson

Contributing Authors

Shanay Lasley

Princess Faith

Te Trice

Angela Lewis

Freda Stevenson

Jacqueline Woodard

Publishing Company: WE Shine Media Solutions
Front/Back Cover Design: Latoya Jackson
Interior Insert Designs: Latoya Jackson
Editing by: WE Shine Media Solutions

ISBN 978-1-312-38813-0

Printed in: The United States, First Edition

Table of Contents

WOMEN™
of Peace

Latoya Jackson and the other authors are sharing their stories of real-life experiences. These women have overcome broken promises, broken hearts, broken friendships, broken marriages, broken families, fear, and low self-esteem. And they are on a new road to recovery and a new journey, called living life again!
LOVE YOURSELF
QUEEN

Latoya J the Loyal Coach

FINDING ME WAS THE BEST PART

LATOYA JACKSON

DEDICATION

First, I want to thank God for keeping me, loving me, and guiding me.

I want to dedicate this book to myself for just listening and obeying God's will and plan for my life. I learned to put myself first and love me more and more each day.

I want to thank my life coaches, my women's group WOP-Women of Peace, and Table Talk for the PUSH. Thank you, Queens!

Thanks to my husband for being my backbone; I couldn't have done this without him. The love and support he shows me daily is speechless. Honey, I love you, always!

Thanks to my sons for pushing me years ago to not give up on myself and them. Alfus and Keifus, I love you both more than you will ever know.

Thanks to my Grammy. I love you, Lia Noel, granny's baby girl.

To my late parents, John and Diane Carr, thank you for giving me life and watching over us. I love and miss you both so much!

I will continue to make you all proud.

Let your Faith be bigger than your fears.
I am so glad I found me.

"Finding Love and Peace Within"

"PEACE WITHIN"
Peace be within you!
Psalm 122:7-8

Introduction
Finding Me Was The Best Part
(Delivered to Deliverance)

A stronghold keeps a person from thinking clearly, accepting the truth, repenting of sins, and receiving deliverance. A stronghold can keep an unbeliever from hearing the good news. A stronghold can keep a believer from hearing the fullness of the good news.

Faith comes by hearing the word of God.
Latoya J the Loyal Coach

Hello Queens, I am Latoya Jackson, a visionary leader passionate about enhancing lives and impacting communities and women through life coaching and personal development. I have always dreamed of becoming a life coach, and I had written in my journal in 2018 that I wanted to write a book. Well, in the year 2020, I did a thing! I became a first-time author of a book called "Broken Crayons Still Color." Then in 2021, I became a certified relationship life coach. It was empowering—manifesting my dreams and becoming an author and life coach. I wanted to empower other women and help them find love and peace within, so my life became busy with pursuing my purpose and my passion.

In 2022 I was in a still season; I had to take a step back and focus on myself. I was leading other women when I wasn't completely healed myself. I recognized it while doing my speaking engagements and women's conferences. I prayed about it and asked God to guide me and show me the way.

For months I didn't do any speaking events, my women's conference had gotten postponed, and I had a few delays in other engagements. It was time to truly focus on myself. Sometimes people think you have to keep moving and stay in the spotlight. Not me. I realized I needed a break in order to be healed! **In 2022, I found myself.**

Finding Me Was The Best Part

Now, I can speak on my journey of finding me and loving me. I put myself first! I started praying more and asking God for clarity in my relationships. I began speaking daily affirmations and putting self-care and self-love before others. Self-care and Self-love are needed! I released all expectations. I began to walk in my full confidence, aligning myself with the universe and the right people. That journey allowed me to know my worth, find love in the things I am passionate about, understand my purpose, walk in my promises, and love ALL of ME. As I began to fill my own cup, the overflow went to loving my husband, loving my two sons, loving my granddaughter, loving my siblings, and loving my family and friends.

God is an on-time God! I'm grateful and thankful that I found me. It required taking a step back to help myself before I could even take a step forward in my life journey to help others. You have to love yourself first and put self-worth first. I had to heal completely and hear from God before I could go on with helping other women overcome their brokenness and fears. I know my purpose is to help those women find love and peace within. Through my life coaching, my goal is to help other women find the woman that they don't see in the mirror. That reflection is the real you! When you look in the mirror, look closely, and you will see the gorgeous Queen that you are. You are beautiful; your smile lights up any room or dark place. As you look in the mirror, say to yourself, I am beautiful, I am loved, and I am a Queen. Embrace that energy and keep smiling and walking in your confidence throughout the day.

**"The biggest lesson I learned is I was already enough."
Tabitha Brown**

During my journey of finding myself and loving myself, I learned to stop being a people pleaser.
The hardest thing I had to do was stop trying to fit in and stop trying to bring everybody with me. My life coach told me that in 2020, however, it was something I had to learn for myself. I wanted to take everybody with me, and I wanted my family and friends to support me. I would get so upset when that didn't happen. I had to realize everybody won't support you and be there to cheer you on, even if you are there to help and support them. In the year 2022, I let go of a lot. No more pleasing people! I chose peace. When you let go of things, God will give you direction and bless you in so many ways!

Thank you, God, for giving me a second chance at life; I'm forever grateful for the many blessings you have placed upon my life. From this day forward, I promise to choose peace, joy, and love over everything! I want to live a happy, blessed, abundant, and fulfilled life. A life with God guiding

11

me and leading me in all the right directions. A faithful,
peaceful, and loving life with my husband, family, and
divine relationships. God, thank you for loving me first.
I love you, God.
Latoya J the Loyal Coach

Stay focused; Focus is the key

Are you motivated? Are you reaching your goals?
Short-term goals and long-term goals are important. Write
those goals down and work towards your goals daily. Get
with those people that will PUSH you and motivate you.
Surround yourself with the right connections and resources.
Remember to pray and speak over your dreams and goals.
Stay focused, and don't let someone else's negative energy
rub off on you.
Surround yourself with positive people and stay focused.
Focus is the key!

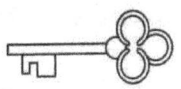

AFFIRMATION
OF Self-Love

I love my life,
I love my body,
I love my eyes,
I love my heart,
I love my sense of humor,
I love my family,
I love to feel inspired,
I love to inspire others,
I love to feel vibrant and
free, I love to dance,
I love to create,
I love to be loved.
I love my SOUL,
I LOVE ME!

Latoya J the Loyal Coach

Tips on How to Become Fearless

Fearlessness is associated with boldness, bravery, and confidence. It allows us to overcome our fears and take chances despite the risk. Fearlessness means acknowledging our fears and doing it nevertheless. Fearlessness means acting despite the odds. It requires trying new things, even if the conclusion is uncertain. Fearlessness requires vulnerability, acceptance of failure, and embracing the unknown. Fearlessness is about growth. Problems should be seen as learning opportunities rather than obstacles to success. Accepting failure as part of learning and using it to succeed is the goal. Fearless does not mean invincible. It involves facing our worries instead of letting them hold us back. It requires us to embrace our fears and just do it! Failure leads to success. It's ok to fail, just don't stay there. You have to keep on PUSHIN!

Three Steps to Becoming Fearless
1. **Acknowledging your worries is the first step to conquering them. Recognize your fears and identify what's stopping you.**
2. **Take small steps. Start with small challenges and work your way up.**
3. **Stay focused. Focus on goals and results and recall your motivation. Remember YOUR why!**

BE FEARLESS!
OVERCOME YOUR FEARS!

Step outside your comfort zone and surround yourself with positive people who will help you overcome your fears and achieve your goals. It's ok that they PUSH you into your greatness.

Take the PUSH!

Remember, you are FEARLESS. Walk in your confidence and own it.

Finding Me Was The Best Part

Everybody has a story; you just gotta be the survivor to tell the story. I came into this world invisible. I overcame some heartaches, brokenness, setbacks, rejections, fears, loneliness, feeling unworthy, not knowing my purpose, and low esteem. I had to take my life back! You fight for what you want and believe in. God, thank you again for a second chance at life. Now I can see, and I am no longer invisible. I was once broken, but I learned that I am worthy and that my life matters. I was broken to become mended. This broken crayon is still coloring, and the broken pieces color just as good and bold.

You can never put something back together that was once broken and make it whole again. However, you can mend the broken pieces back together and make it look just as good. It will never be the same, like broken marriages, broken relationships, heartaches, abandonment, and unfaithfulness, but you can make it better if it's meant to be.

It's ok to mend the broken pieces, just leave the shattered pieces where they are and live now and for the moment. But first, you have to forgive yourself and forgive the person that hurt you.

Even though you are mended back together, you can still live a whole life. I had to find myself in the broken pieces, but now my life has been mended back together, and I am forever grateful. Leave the past in the past and live your life peacefully. God's grace and mercy have kept me whole. Queens, I pray that nothing is broken or missing in your heart or life. You can mend a broken heart and find love and peace within. Have faith and trust in God.

Daily Affirmations

I am beautiful.

I am enough.

I am free.

I am brilliant.

I am powerful.

I am healthy.

I am wealthy.

I am worthy.

I am smart.

I am loved.

I am liked.

I am favored.

I am blessed.

I am thankful.

I am grateful.

I am vibrant and creative.

I believe in myself.

I choose to be happy; everything I need is within me.
I am strong!
I am who I am; I am me.
Life is a journey, and only you hold the key!

Latoya J the Loyal Coach

DAILY AFFIRMATIONS

I believe in me.   I am beautiful.

I am enough.   I am free.

I am brilliant.   I am powerful.

I am healthy.   I am wealthy.

I am worthy.   I am smart.

I am loved.   I am liked.

I am favored.

I choose to be HAPPY, everything I

NEED is within ME.

I am strong!

Abundance is my birthright.

I allow myself to be great

I am who, I am, I am me!

AFFIRMATIONS FOR RELATIONSHIPS

I am worthy of beautiful friendships and lasting relationships.

I am surrounded by people who love me just as I am.

I find love everywhere I look and go.

My presence is delightful to others.

I am loved for all flaws and imperfections.

I deserve a partner who loves, honor, and respects me!
Thank you, Honey for loving me... My wonderful and amazing
husband Kevin, I love you.

No matter what always respect one another and treat each other
with respect and dignity.

I am worthy of being cherished, treasured, and adored.

I am worthy of true and forever lasting love.

Unconditional love is my birthright.

You don't need no one giving you validation in your marriage or
relationships.

I am free to be my true and authentic self in my relationships.

My relationships are fun, joyful, and rooted in pure love.

Love is my birthright, and I will not settle for less than I
deserve.

Latoya J the Loyal Coach

BIO
LATOYA CARR JACKSON

Latoya Carr Jackson was born in Springfield, TN. She is a wife, mother of two sons, and grandmother to a beautiful granddaughter, Lia Noel. Latoya loves to cater, decorate, and make things beautiful. It is a true passion! Latoya's purpose in life is to help women and men overcome broken relationships and to help them find love and peace within.

Latoya loves to laugh and have fun with her family and friends. She loves to help in her community by giving back and helping others. Her Hobbies are crafts, cooking, traveling, decorating, walking in the park, shopping, and journaling.

Latoya went to Springfield High School in Springfield, TN. She went to Tennessee Health Careers and received her CNA license in 2011. She stepped out on FAITH and started a catering and decorating business the same year. Latoya is currently in her 12th year of business. Her catering and decorating business is Your Cost Catering & Events Decor, which is located in Springfield, TN.

Latoya is a mentor, natural-born leader, certified relationship life coach, author, motivational speaker, and leader of two Women's groups in Springfield, TN. She is the co-founder of W2W- Woman 2 Woman and founder of WOP- Women of Peace. Latoya loves to inspire and help others overcome things and push them to keep going in life.

She is empowered by the love she gives and receives from her mentors. Latoya is loving and very caring to everyone she meets.

https://linktr.ee/toyakj1

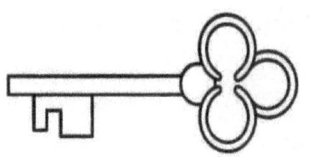

Latoya J the Loyal Coach

Finding Love and

Peace Within.

MY ANSWERED PRAYER
SHANAY LASLEY

DEDICATION

I dedicate this to my three reasons to keep going: TJ, Rickey, and Jada. I love each of you beyond this life.

To my parents, I can't thank you enough for loving me through it all; God blessed me with angels. My grandparents in heaven were the blueprint.

Aunt Darlene, you are my gatekeeper and treasure.

Aunt Paulette, you lit my path in dark places and caught flights to catch my tears.

Tashia, your love and support is my strength.

Twin, thank you for the shift.

Deb, thank you for the covering.

Queen Brooklyn Tankard, you were the vessel that propelled my purpose.

Queen Latoya Jackson, thank you for believing in my gifts.

Darcy, your calling is evident, and your support produces needed revelation.

My anointed Pastor Tony McGee, your leadership is my life support.

To my family & friends, I love you all until the end.

And to my Answered Prayer....Romans 8:28.

To God be the glory for all he has done.

Blessings Always,

Shanay Lasley

DISCLAIMER**

The author has made every effort to ensure the accuracy of the information within this chapter was correct at the time of publication. The author does not assume and hereby disclaims any liability to any party for any loss, damage, or disruption caused by errors or omissions, whether such errors or omissions result from accident, negligence, or any other cause. The story told is the author's version of the events as they took place. The author recognizes that other people's memories of the events described in this chapter may be different than their own. The details are not intended to hurt, offend or defame anyone.

All poems are original works of Shanay Lasley

My Answered Prayer

Freedom...

"Freedom is never free" ~Maya Angelou

I don't know about you, but I have struggled with being bold with my gifts. I have always loved to write poetry but felt it was just a cathartic outlet for me. It was something personal that I could share with family and friends, never thinking my pain and passion on paper could actually translate into healing for others. It's freeing to finally give my anguish a platform.

People say, "Just do it scared." Well, that is precisely what I'm doing right now. Scared as hell, nevertheless, I am stepping out on faith bolder than ever and asking God to help me execute whatever gifts he has given me and use them for the greater good. After all, the old adage is that God doesn't call the qualified; He qualifies the called. The good Lord will have to qualify me because I'm no expert. I'm just a woman who has experienced a few things and decided to step out on faith this time. My daughter Jada said, "When we take chances, either nothing will happen, or everything will."

This life of mine hasn't been easy, but it hasn't been the worst either. I know plenty of people that have gone through a lot worse than me. Who am I to question the trials I go through, especially when I brought most of them on myself? Yep, I said it; the first step to recovery is admitting it, and I admit I have driven myself into a wall many times. I drove right off of the decision cliff, despite flashing do not enter signs, and I had the audacity to question the Creator, who has the hindsight and foresight on everything I face. Yet, I ignored the whispers and sometimes the bullhorn.

The crazy thing is that the repercussions are usually always worse than being obedient the first time. If I had to do it over, I would've listened to the many voices that offered sound instruction. You cannot live outside the will of God and yet want the will of God for your life. This is what I had to learn the hard way. Learning to hear from God means that he may not always tell you what you want to hear, just like a good parent protecting their child.

My story isn't unfamiliar to most. I have survived some painful things in my life. Anyone who knows me knows I struggled with survivor's remorse after losing my only younger sibling TJ to leukemia in 1996. Honestly, there isn't a day that goes by that I don't miss my brother or think about how different my life would be had he survived. I tried everything I could to protect my brother, even donating my bone marrow to him in an attempt to extend his life. Losing him left me numb, angry, confused, and devastated. This was a two-year emotional roller coaster of hospital stays, spinal taps, chemotherapy, sleepless nights, and tumultuous trauma.

We watched him lose weight, hair, and strength, but he never lost hope. My brother never complained; he just fought for his life. TJ would also bounce in and out of remission, which had all of us hanging on to hope. It was a very traumatic experience. After the loss, some of my family lashed out, not knowing how to channel their frustration and pain, which caused some division in our tribe. This often stems from the death of a loved one; however, no matter how many people tried to console me, it left me feeling isolated and angry. I would ask myself, how are you mad when I lost *my* only baby brother, and my parents lost *their* only son?

The truth is, we were all hurting. They say that anger is easier to deal with than pain; I can attest to that. I internalized a lot of the hurt and blamed myself. If I had dealt with my grief head-on, maybe I would've made more sound decisions; only God knows. I grieved T for a very long time and still do. Honestly, I didn't think I deserved to be "spared" because, in my mind, he wasn't. That was the beginning of my spiritual demise. This poem gives a glimpse into my life after losing my brother and what my life resembled. It's not pretty; in fact, you may think like Twin once told me…that you just saw me naked. "Freedom" digs deep into a part of me that needed healing, revelation, deliverance, and self-love…well, welcome to my truth in words…

POEM: Freedom

Engaging because something in ME is changing. My contentment suddenly turned into resentment, and I am finally bold enough to admit it.

They say Love doesn't cost a thing, but it cost me Freedom. It cost me consciousness; it cost me peace of mind and love that I can truly call MINE.

I have allowed love to use me, abuse me, and strip me of my dignity. I have made too many mistakes to count, feeling like love was something cheap, so just go ahead and pass it out. Forsake me for all others tattooed in my heart, a fool I was because red flags no longer mimicked doubt.

Just call me toxic because I can't block this behavior out. Why am I still here? Oh, that's right, I allowed THIS so-called "love thang" to replace my fear. I felt paralyzed, stuck on stupid call me Nike, just do it …

Why do I play myself, degrade myself, put my heart on clearance like your cheap shoes…what spell is this? What the hell is this?…felt like heaven at the time just because your weak ass decided to blow my mind with words cheap

28

as your shoes...no depth cause low self-esteem doesn't require a narcissist to come correct.

That's my fault; I didn't even see the clearance tag hanging on me like a damn Charlie Brown Christmas tree, missing essentials. Be essential, walk in a room, command respect - PRESIDENTIAL is how I was raised, but somehow, the wolves got to me; I lost myself when we lost T.

I left me to be unprotected and redirected down the wrong path. What did I care? My little brother is no longer here; I don't deserve that love...the love that T deserved to see...so it can be free to the most qualified toxic male out there.

Somehow, I normalized drowning as long as my family was happy and smiling ...their smiles outweighed my common sense... ever since I lost my smile.

Use me; verbally, financially, and mentally abuse me...seemed ok at the time, as long as the disguise came with charm at the drop of a dime.

Losing my childhood friend Bryan was another blow, but this time I saw my life run in my mind REAL slow.... he died pleasing everyone else but himself, am I next miserable laid to rest?

God help me, please; this situation is bringing me straight to my knees. Laying this at your feet, please allow me to be still in this season of reasoning. Help me muster up more courage and faith than the mustard seed you say can save me.

When I wake up from this bad dream, please allow my new reality to reflect a new reflection of me; let love flow the way it should, ordained and free of past life toxic stains.

Baptize me, brand new full of clarity, and still some familiarity so I can still recognize me. I don't want to lose myself and abuse myself ever again.

They say love doesn't cost a thing, but THIS time, mine WILL come with a price. Align with the Creator, seek him in all things, and make sure critical decisions are made with precision..... So, the next time that flag is thrown at me, I can discern with concern because my Freedom means more to me than your DISINGENUOUS toxic needs. I have finally decided to choose ME, cause Real Freedom is not Free...

~ Shanay Lasley

~~~~~~

Bad Decisions...

"Bad decisions made with good intentions are still bad decisions" ~James C. Collins

Ahh, real freedom did come with a cost. Deaf ears silenced the truth, and this expensive mistake resulted from some reckless choices, choices for which I have asked God to forgive me. If you were ever affected by any of my bad decisions, I ask that you forgive me too. If I'm honest, I also had to forgive myself. I said, "I do," being rebellious and disobedient. I'm still paying for it (literally), but some of the most beautiful things have a hefty price tag, and the freedom that my soul needed was priceless.

That toxic situation ended, and my journey to healing and self-discovery began. It cost me financially, spiritually, mentally, and emotionally, but like my dad says, "You will bounce back." He also said kids and family don't have a choice, but we choose our partners, so choose wisely. I have apologized to my kids and parents for *that* bad choice. They are so loving and accepting; all they ever wanted was to see me happy.

I learned that picking the wrong person takes your children and family through your trauma, and it's certainly not fair to them. I realized that I took on some of *his* trauma that wasn't even my own. Unintentional trauma is *still* trauma. Your issues can spill over to your loved ones that want to protect you. Wanting to "fix" him was my biggest mistake. You can't people check like spellcheck; it never ends well. I'm thankful my family loves me unconditionally as I do them.

Healing from trauma doesn't just stop overnight; it takes work, yet peeling back the layers to uncover low self-esteem and self-worth forces a necessary vulnerability. I couldn't relegate my decisions to anyone else; it was poor judgment and lack of discernment on my part. Mistakes can be very costly, but they can also develop strength, character, and a resilience like you've never known. I will never mention his name because that may cost me too; however, I will say, yes, you can drink from a broken glass but don't be shocked when it cuts you.

Part of growth is pruning, and I had to go to the places in me that needed answers - the places that were void of clarity and intuition. Learning to recognize brokenness is first ensuring that you are healed and whole enough to do so. I know I am not the only one that allowed an opportunist to come in and "opportune"....I held so much anger inside from the outcome of this train wreck of a union, yet the one I needed to blame was staring back at me in the mirror.

I had to learn that I don't have to entertain everything I attract. I had to own my part in being hasty and feeling like nothing better would come along. I had to own the fact that I didn't trust God enough, and my faith was feeble. For me, saying "I messed up" preceding judgment freed some of the shame I faced. After all, I have to look at myself in the mirror, and there is a freedom that comes from admitting flaws. My brother from another mother, Darcy, told me to start saying these two words to myself and out loud…SO WHAT! Yes, I made mistakes; who doesn't? So, what! Yes, I chose wrong, so what? Yes, I haven't always had it all figured out…so what…God still loves me, and he is a God of second chances…multiple chances. That, my friends, is freedom.

Lesson… trust God to order your steps.

Sometimes God moves, and other times, he waits on us to move. It seems like God does his best work when we get still and allow his will to be done.

"God will order your steps; you just need to move your feet," said my Aunt Emma as we discussed the importance of path and purpose.

"There is no need to hurry what the maker has already written," my mom says.

Trusting the process sometimes means accepting outcomes that look nothing like what we planned or envisioned but knowing that it will all work together for our greater good. (Romans 8:28) Nope, I can't preach a sermon (yet), but I can refer to the Word for guidance and revelation. I was raised as a believer, and I lean on my faith now more than ever. It is literally the air that I breathe. I don't make a move without talking it over with God and then getting still like a kid in the time-out corner of a classroom.

You see, God was talking to me through people and circumstances for a long time, but I was ignorant to his call.

I wanted to take shortcuts, do what I wanted to do, and then pray about it. That is the most backward way to think. It's like attempting to assemble something that has tons of pieces and putting it together all wrong, and THEN sitting down to read the instructions.

Lesson...seeking God *after* the debauchery can cost you years that can't be recovered.

That has been my life up until now. My faith was in dire need of resuscitation. I had to wait until the big age I am now to figure out that I was working extra hard for no reason. In hindsight, God was talking to me the whole time; I just wasn't in the right faith space to receive his directive. Let me explain. Faith space to me is being in a place of stillness and waiting on God to give instruction by allowing things to take place in our lives. Sitting in a faith space can be scary and unpredictable. Hebrews 11:6 says, "*And without faith it is impossible to please Him, for he who comes to God must believe that He is and that He is a rewarder of those who seek Him.*"

Simply put, stepping out on faith means total trust in God regardless of the outcome. He is the author and finisher, period. I had to lean into this and practice it daily. I still do, and when I fall, I ask the Creator to help me with my weakness. If I'm real, sometimes I beg God for clarity, cry out in frustration, sit praying in my closet, fall asleep with tears drenching my pillow, or all the above. Prayer is a command and practice; it's sacred to me now. Although it's exhausting at times, that purge of emotion is also the most liberating.

My newfound faith space has transformed how I deal with all adversity I face. My brother from another mother, Darcy, told me recently, "Because your pain is real, your praise will be real." I stand on God's promise that he will never leave or forsake me (Deuteronomy 31:8). I truly believe that God is with me.

Lesson…epiphanies only happen when we are ready to receive them.

As my Pastor explained, "God gives us free will to connect with him. He is a constant even when we are not. We have to flip the switch that activates his power in our lives."

It's a choice I now consider a privilege because I have seen him perform miracles in my life and in the lives of people I know and love.

Boundaries…

"Don't say maybe if you want to say no." ~Paulo Coelho

Boundary:

Be aware

Of what is

Unacceptable and

Normalize saying no

Do what is best for you

And know it's not your

Responsibility to sacrifice

Yourself for others

(OurMindfulLife.co)

Fragile Faith…

"Only in the darkness can you see the stars" ~ Dr. Martin Luther King, Jr.

34

There I was, sitting in my car, crying my eyes out because I was so frustrated with where my relationship was headed. I made a frantic call to my Pastor, and what he told me was supposed to be my ah-ha moment and my out...this was the bullhorn I mentioned earlier... (I had so many sirens I could've patented one). He said in the most profound yet gentle way..." You already know what to do." That was the day I heard from God, but I ignored his voice. In other words, if I were anchored in my faith and praying like I should've been, the decision would've been made **that day**. However, my faith was so fragile that I allowed the enemy to dictate my direction.

Lesson…. if you are uneasy and your partner is forever unbothered, that is a problem.

"Fair exchange has never been any robbery" ~Grandma Cunningham

A relationship takes two (three when God-centered). I vividly remember saying that if I'm not okay, then "we're" not supposed to be okay…okay??? Well, the response I would get is... "That's YOU…I'm good." Stop right there is what I should've done. I replayed so many scenarios in my head over and over, wondering how I allowed this to happen. What was I thinking?

There I was, nervous, anxious, confused, and doubtful if I was doing the right thing. After all, the kids seemed happy, and my parents were good... well, as long as I was. Let me tell you something, when family and friends love you, they will let you wear the clown face if you refuse to take it off and be on standby with makeup remover when you have had enough. I spent all this money to look beautiful on that day, invested all these years, surely crossing this finish line was the last step in the order of business, right? Wrong!

Some adults still deal with infancy issues, and if left unresolved, that childhood trauma can spill over into their relationships and affect the person they coexist with. You will find yourself dealing with their trauma. What is worse is they don't even recognize there is a problem because they have normalized toxic behavior and patterns. I heard someone say you may marry someone for how they look but will end up divorcing them for how they think…. Touché. Multiple memories and years mean absolutely nothing with the *wrong one*.

Lesson…. you can be a secure individual in an insecure relationship; do not convince yourself, or, more importantly, do not let anyone else convince you otherwise.

If pleasing others corrupts your character, mutilates your mindset, and stains your soul, then it is a **BIG NO**. No, I don't have to entertain your shenanigans….No, I am not comfortable doing this just to please you…. No, you can no longer disrespect me, and in the words of my mentor and good sis Latoya ..…NO is a complete sentence, period! What?! Can I get an amen y'all?!

(1 Corinthians 15:33) *"Bad company corrupts good character."*

Lesson… being in a relationship with someone that has nothing to lose can cause you to lose everything.

Here I was, going from therapist to therapist, thinking something was wrong with me…well, it was…I didn't understand the power that I held inside of me. I was looking for answers, yet had I just sat still with God, I would've gained the confidence and wisdom I needed to walk away long before I did.

"Trust in the Lord; everything else will follow," said my Aunt Darlene.

36

Fragile faith will have your mind wrapped like flimsy tape. All I had to do was trust God with my entire being, but that takes spiritual maturity. Honestly, it is not easy; it takes surrender. It's a daily walk, talk, and purge with the Lord. I had to learn how to be intimate with God on a deeper level and connect with the one that knows me better than I know myself. I had to invite the Lord into my heart for good. The enemy had me convinced that the odds of finding someone else to spend my life with were slim to none.

Lesson…however God wants me to spend the rest of my life is his business when I trust his will.

Read that again! Oh man, I wish I had this mindset before saying I do to Mr. I don't. The most important person you can ever let down is yourself. I had to learn this the hard way, hence why everyone is not equipped to be your purpose partner. Just like seasonal jobs, some relationships are seasonal and temporary. There are people that literally prey on your vulnerabilities and don't care about you losing you along with all you have as long as they are gaining everything *they* want. The bottom line is this… I abandoned myself. I committed myself to someone that didn't commit to God before committing to me.

Part of self-care is respecting yourself enough even when others don't respect you. I cannot believe I co-signed my own disrespect. Allowing someone with questionable character and morals to devalue me was playing Russian roulette with my soul. This awesome yet painful reflection is impactful and necessary. Being transparent before someone else can point out your flaws is extremely liberating. No one is above fragility. I have become a professional at pointing the finger at myself, so there is no need to run pass interference on my mistakes.

"Remain Teachable."~Aunt Paulette

Getting a handle on my life meant surrender. I will say that again and again… surrendering to God is the greatest gift to yourself. It allows alignment and peace; it allows grace and acceptance. It also allows forgiveness to enter into the rigid places of the heart.

Lord, please help me forgive those who attempted to rob me of the joy you give freely. Your sovereignty is my strength and safe place. Thank you for the peace you have given me in accepting my brother's transition. In your promise is where I hide and continue to heal. Amen

POEM: Dear God

Thank you for the lessons that didn't kill me. Those predestined scars healed me.

In some ways, some days I just exist until I enlist your voice …Jesus, I need you, sitting at your feet…I bleed too, not Calvary, but what was missing in me…

GPS…God Provides that Safety net when I ball, when I fall, when I crawl. Not out of the womb but from these wounds… A simple thank you turned into countless IOUs…

I ain't felt right, lots of sleepless nights…cried myself to sleep, conversations with you ran so deep… can't do life without you…

I've been a fool, happy, miserable. I broke a lot of rules…traded meditation for temptation…did I mention tragedy & trouble got my attention? So sorry, God, I'm listening…. back to the bricks my grandma laid for me. She swore I'd need you; that angel prayed for me…greatest gift she gave me was YOU.

Even when I played, I prayed & even when I strayed, YOU stayed a constant in my life…undeserving, yet you still

carry me on those sleepless nights. Unconditional when I'm hypocritical...life has been unkind...your love transcends my sins...unbelievably unbreakable bond, I am yours, and you are mine...

God, can you hear me? Please stay near me... these tests are getting harder; cover my kids. Please protect my son & daughter...cause this world is cruel...let them know your grace will be sufficient. When they're deficient in direction, they, too, will require your love & protection to resuscitate them when they bleed.

Life's biggest misconception is there is no need for YOU...please walk with me and talk with me until my spirit meets with you. IOU everything and more so when I enter Heaven's door and fall at your feet... I pray you see humility. God...You saved me....

~ Shanay Lasley

Lesson.... snatch your power back; it's yours.

"When you wake up to your power and snatch it back, miracles happen." ~Lalah Delia

"Doing the right thing for the wrong reason is treason against yourself," is a quote by the poet T.S. Eliot. Twin uttered those words to me in a moment of decision that shifted the entire trajectory of my life. That was the moment I knew I had given my power away, and it was time to get it back. I thought I was doing the right thing, but I wasn't happy. My happiness was seeing my loved ones happy, even if it meant I was settling. Sis.... let me tell you, DON'T SETTLE!! (Great read, by the way, Judge Faith Jenkins). You deserve to have the same smile on your face as your kids and family. If you are not happy, that fraudulent relationship will not last; if it's not organic, it is not sustainable.

Lesson…. if there is constant chaos, trust issues, insecurities, and disrespect, and you know if you had a way out, you would take it…. then it's time to pray, prepare, and proceed.

Trying to do things the right way shouldn't compromise your happiness and peace of mind. Listen to that voice, those whispers, and if it is full of negativity, it will stay that way, but you don't have to. Life and death truly do reside with our words. Psalm 37:4, *"God will give you the desires of your heart."* Plot twist… sometimes those desires come with tough decisions; triumphs come with tests, breakthroughs come with breakdowns, and elevation comes with exodus.

"We serve a God of suddenly." ~Princess Faith

Leaving those things which are familiar, i.e., abuse, toxic relationships, chaos, and confusion, requires a changed mindset. I didn't pick up my bed per se…but I did grab my purse and GO! Sure, there were some good days, but dancing with the devil is fun, too, until those horns rear their ugly head. You have to give yourself the gift of goodbye! Saying goodbye to your old self is saying enough is truly enough, and you deserve better.

Sadly, I knew I deserved better while saying I do, but that whisper said I don't. I don't know if I can trust you isn't the smartest way to enter any relationship. I walked away from years of mixed signals and mess with nothing but the clothes on my back. I felt like Angela Bassett in Waiting to Exhale...Chile, all I needed was a cigarette and lighter fluid. But on a serious note, it was time. Time for me to trust God with my life, what was left of it anyway.

"My Father in heaven is the overflow; all you have to do is ask for it." Aunt Polly

Like everything in life, even that relationship had a purpose; it catapulted me to this defining moment. This moment in time is glorious. I am falling in love with who I was meant to be, a strong woman of faith and purpose. The daughter my parents raised to know better, the sister my little brother would be proud of, and a mother that her children can look up to.

Lesson… *"Let God handle your problems while you tend to your purpose" ~ Shanay Lasley*

POEM: Mask Off

Step from behind the mask…why you ask? Cause these wounds, my war room holds names and faces…I dare not erase the dark places where I walked through the valley of the shadows…it's easy to stray there but death is when you stay there…. self-destruction never plays fair.

Painful divorce, lost my only sibling, little brotha…survivor's remorse…questionable decisions…if you could see my spiritual incisions…you wouldn't recognize me.

Toxic is the new temptation that will devour our gut instincts, revelation after revelation. Gratitude to the Most High…I died to flesh a thousand times…solid mental health is the real bag and the new wealth.

I prayed for peace; trauma ran deep…most was self-inflicted for entertaining the enemy's sheep…simply put…ignoring red flags was never a good look…

I thought I was damaged until I managed to realize that my purpose ain't perfect…everything I overcame was worth it to birth this!!! My platform is to inform…no more wasted time…Once I valued my worth…I came to reclaim what's mine!!! Setting healthy boundaries, letting go, and being ok with saying NO!!! I found a new love, and her name is ME!!!

Behind the mask...self-validation is key...fill your own cup. I am worthy...I am Enough! I am Free, I am her, and she is beautifully imperfect. Mask Off. She is healed; she is ME...

~ Shanay Lasley

BIO

SHANAY LASLEY

Shanay is a poet, author, and proud mother of two children, Rickey and Jada. She was born and raised in Indianapolis, Indiana. She holds an Associate's Degree in Human Resource Management and a Bachelor's Degree in Business Administration from Marian University.

She is a member of the African American Special Emphasis Program, which promotes diversity and inclusion in all aspects of leadership development and equal opportunity. She also participates in the Women's Shelter Initiative. This awesome initiative promotes programs that aid women and children to stabilize themselves successfully back into society post-abuse, amongst other interrelated issues. Shanay is passionate about pursuing her purpose to help those who, like herself, struggle with getting out of their own way.

She has weathered many storms in her life, including the devastating loss of her only sibling TJ to leukemia when he was just 17 years old. Although many tragic events unfolded, those valley moments are what helped strengthen her faith in God.

Shanay has always considered writing to be extremely therapeutic and is finally brave enough to share her story. These valley moments did not break her; they shaped her. God has ordered her steps, and now Shanay is simply moving her feet.

Shanay Lasley

Email: NAY32298@yahoo.com

IG: **TJSIS625**

Facebook: Shanay Lasley

Twitter: @shan69916

Finding Love and
Peace Within.

LOVE AND PEACE ARE JOURNEYS, NOT A DESTINATION

PRINCESS FAITH

DEDICATION

I dedicate my writings to all the unheard and unhealed little girls that live inside the darkest corners of our minds.

LOVE AND PEACE ARE JOURNEYS,

NOT A DESTINATION

*Sometimes Deciding Who You Are Means Deciding Who
You Will Never Be Again*

~ Tiny Buddha~

An Open Letter to The Demons I Left Behind

Where do I begin? We haven't spoken in so long, and after
this letter is done, we won't speak again. I ask that you not
torture the souls that remain in the past, who still blame me
for a love lost from relationships that did not last or from
friendships they feel ended too soon. What they didn't
understand was that I wasn't leaving them; I was leaving
you. Your shape shifted and took many forms, showing up
as deceit, unaccountability, abandonment, lack of effort,
and/or empathy, as well as so many other things. Help them
understand that because you held them close was the reason
I couldn't keep them close to me.

There was a vision given—a mission to be fulfilled. The
task given to me I accepted at will. It was on the journey
that I shed all the emotions those memories bring, like hurt,
shame, and guilt, to lighten the load as I changed. Please
tell them that I sincerely apologize for the pain I caused as I
was living in my own. There was just no way I could live
on in that space in time. It was life or death for me. I had to
move on to survive.

We're in two different worlds now, and although we no
longer align, I still hold them dear, and they're still great in

my eyes. So please leave them alone now. Let their weary souls rest. Let them know that they're enough, and I know they gave their best. It's okay to let go. You know, live and let live. Just because I let go doesn't mean I don't have love for them still. To learn to forgive me the way I had to forgive them, unconditionally without apology, just understanding it was God's will. Last but certainly not least, I pray they'll find peace and appreciate the good, the bad, and the indifferent when they think of me.

~~~ Princess Faith ~~~

When I wrote the aforementioned poem, I was offering up a cry out to those dark forces that kept people I had encountered on my life journey bound while I had taken a different route and chose to take a path of healing. I had grown tired of those I chose to leave behind, trying to use the snares of guilt and shame as a net to capture my momentum and drag me down to where they believed I should be. They identified with the demons I no longer embraced, and due to their comfort in their company, the same people were not willing to accept my need for change.

Life is a journey to which we are only provided one admission ticket. Much like any other journey, there will be pit stops along the way. Some stops are filled with beautiful atmospheric scenery that can't be captured. Those are the places that you would physically have to be there to gain full appreciation. We tend to stop for just a while. Long enough to take in the site to say we've had the privilege of the scenery but not quite long enough to get to know the history behind it. Then there are stops that are needed. We refer to this as a rest stop. It may be to refuel because the gas is low, catch a quick nap, take a walk and stretch a bit, or just empty waste from our bodies, all in the name of preparing ourselves to continue down the road.

Then there are unplanned stops. This is when something unexpected has occurred due to improper preparation or hazards on the road. When this form of stop occurs, it causes a disturbance in our journey. We are thrown into a position where we have to deviate from the original plan and make tough decisions to avoid becoming stuck in that place. We are armed with this knowledge; however, many do not exercise the wisdom to connect this practical information to everyday life. Nowhere is this more evident than in the life of an unhealed soul.

We all have that person we never want to ride with because we know they will make too many stops, and we want to get to the destination. Well, my path would be that driver. My life was filled with pit stops. It took me 43 years to realize that I had never quite lived but had, in fact, only been surviving. I was a world traveler, highly awarded professional nurse, accomplished entrepreneur, and philanthropist, all while feeling like an unfulfilled soul. I was happy and living the life I chose, financially stable enough to walk away from a six-figure career in nursing, spend some time abroad, and make some great connections along the way.

As far as I was concerned, I had escaped the severe effects of childhood trauma that tends to cripple so many in their adult lives. The rape, the incest, and the emotional, mental and spiritual abuse had been left in the shadows of my memories, never to rise again. I thought I had arrived until my journey led me to this amazing soul named Shadawn, who, through our sisterhood, had the ability to expose me to me. I had been riding the waves of success when an unexpected event provided a need in my life, to which she immediately and readily stepped in to be a covering.

We spent a few days together, which provided the space for long deep conversations. The mask began to come off piece by piece. I was forced to confront internal pain that I had suppressed in order to survive and keep pushing forward. The one that surfaced first was the summer of "21," but first, let's revisit the year prior. This was when I encountered the most significant hazard in my life journey to date. Up until that point, I thought nothing could ever come close to the anguish I experienced in January 2020.

It was the start of a new year. I was employed by one of our generation's top pop R&B artists and days away from the launch of my first published book titled "In The Shade of the Apple Tree." The love of my life, a fireman and first responder from my hometown of Nashville, TN, was a go-getter like me and understood my demanding schedule as a healthcare professional. He treated me really well, and everything about us just worked. I was enjoying life to its fullest.

On January 26th of the year 2020, it all changed. The world was awakened to the news that Kobe Bryant and eight others had lost their lives in a helicopter crash. I was glued to the television when my phone kept ringing. I hesitated to answer, believing it was just someone ready to discuss this tragic event. I picked up my phone, however, when I noticed a notification from a dear friend in ST. Croix. This particular friend only called when it was emergent, so I knew to answer. It turns out she was calling to notify me that my best friend had passed away unexpectedly. I was distraught. It was a heavy day with all the sad news.

The entire day was spent trying to process my emotions, and before I laid down to bed, I picked up the phone to call my boyfriend again since I had been calling all day with no response. I wasn't particularly concerned because I trusted him. As I climbed into bed, I decided to scroll through social media as a distraction from the day's events. Little did I know that the dark energy that hung over me that day was not yet done. As I continued to scroll through my timeline, I happened to catch my man, who I saw as my best friend, hugged up with another woman and toasting to who knows what. It had been posted on a mutual friend's timeline.

I quickly went to my boyfriend's page, but there was no evidence of any such thing there, so I went back to the mutual friend's page and watched the video again to confirm that my eyes had not deceived me. There it was for all the world to see. My heart was shattered. To make matters worse, I received a call that my grandmother had been rushed to the hospital and wasn't expected to make it through the night. I grabbed my keys, hopped on the highway, and headed straight home to Nashville.

My mind was racing a thousand miles an hour. What was an average 3 ½ hour drive only took me about 2 hours and 45 minutes to make as I raced 90 miles an hour north on I-75 in my midsized sedan. My heart was screaming, but my voice was silent as tears flowed down my face. How much more could I take? I was angry. I was confused. I was hurt. This had to be an alternate reality. In a matter of hours, the world had significantly altered three of my four most significant foundational relationships.

I reached Antioch first, where my mother and my boyfriend both owned homes exactly one mile apart. Pulling over to the gas station that sat halfway between my mother's home and his, I called my boyfriend again, and he finally picked up. I was so upset that I just started screaming as tears poured down my face. He suggested I meet him at his house. I told him I had to check on my grandmother first, and then I'd be over. I drove to Skyline Medical Center, where my grandmother had been admitted and was now stabilized. I spent some time with her before leaving to talk with my boyfriend face-to-face.

We talked without any clear answers from him as to who this other woman was or how this had happened. The only information he would offer was that she would meal prep for the guys at the fire hall. In the moments when I couldn't find words to say, he would ask me to talk to him and tell him how I felt. It was hurtful to be asked such a question after he expressed to me that he loved both of us but for different reasons. He asked me not to be mad at him. I was lost between trying to be strong and fighting for what my heart desired. I found myself standing in the middle of his kitchen where we had made so many wonderful memories begging a man who had just cheated on me to love me. I felt like I was in the middle of a sick game.

Leaving his house, I drove back to the hospital, where my emotional state was evident to everyone. I was standing at my grandmother's bedside when she looked at me and stated, "Princess Faith, I haven't seen you this broken since you were a child." I looked at the clock, thinking how it was now January 27th, the birthday of the only sibling I had ever lost, and my heart broke a little more, reminiscing on how I missed my brother.

I silently walked out of the room and made my way to the hospital parking lot, where I sat in my car for 10 hours, perfectly still in silence, trying to process the previous 24 hours of my life. I was frozen and could not move. I didn't want to go anywhere or be around anyone. I had never felt that level of pain before. I had experienced great trauma throughout life, but this was different. This time I had been violated by someone who offered no sign of his hidden red flags. I felt foolish. After surviving a severely traumatic marriage just a few years prior, I never thought I would allow such vulnerability in my life again. Yet here I was.

Over the next few days, I spent the night with my boyfriend, aware that it was over and uncertain about what I expected to happen or what I wanted moving forward. I was simultaneously fighting for us and yielding to the need to let him be free to choose without guilt where he wanted to be. The entire situation was overwhelming. I eventually drove to the other woman's house to get the answers I was seeking.

There we were face to face. She was shorter than me, walked with a slight limp in her step, and had an older appearance. I sat there listening as she informed me she had been seeing my boyfriend for six months by that point and that he had told her he was in love with her. She spoke to him every day and had met his two daughters and their mother, as well as often spent time with his mother. She further informed me he had rented the Nashville fireman union hall to host her mother's birthday party just a few months prior in October. That was the final blow as I recalled how he had canceled his trip with me to New York during the same dates that she stated her mother's party had taken place.

As hard as it was to hear another woman tell me everything that she shared with me on that day, I listened. I continued to listen as she stated that he knew she was messing around with three men at that time but didn't care and that her daughters would caution her that he was moving too fast and didn't trust him. I stood there outside her home and listened, wondering why he would choose a 40+ woman who bragged about playing men because "they were like fleas, and she played them before they had a chance to play her." Why would he choose that mindset over a faithful and ambitious successful woman he was already in a relationship with?

I allowed her the space to tell me everything that she wanted to say. I then called him up in front of her, which led to me screaming in anger again. She asked me if she could speak to him, to which I obliged her request before abruptly ending the call and leaving. I drove back to Atlanta to prepare to fly to the USVI for my best friend's funeral. I spent the next week relaxing on the islands as I prepared for her final arrangements. Upon leaving the Virgin Islands, I flew to Los Angeles to work on a client's project.

While I was in the Caribbean, my book was released, which included a full-page dedication to my boyfriend. This added to the very public embarrassment he had already caused me throughout the ordeal, so my week in California became a needed escape. I climbed Runyon Mountain every morning, which took a few hours to reach the top and back down. So many times, I wanted to stop on the way up, but something inside me would not let me quit. I told myself that if I could just push through and reach the top, I could push through anything life threw at me.

Once I made it to the top, I realized that the trail back down the mountain was vastly different. It wasn't the same smooth pavement I had walked to the top. It was rugged, unpaved, and narrow. I recall being afraid to take the first step when God spoke to me, saying, "Princess Faith, I'm with you. Everyone isn't equipped to take this road, nor will everyone take the same steps to the finish line. Daughter, you will be okay. I know it looks rough, but it's all about finding your path down." I inhaled deeply and took my first few steps. I decided to trust in his word to guide me through.

After accomplishing my goal, I went back to the mountain every day I was there. By day 3, I was racing through the path. God had shown me his faithfulness, and I improved daily. The only time I felt relief from the pain was when I was on the mountain. It was in this that I learned to welcome the mountains when they showed up in my life.

I would video call my grandmother to keep up to date on her status and find comfort in hearing her voice. I promised her I'd be to see her when I left the west coast. After flying to my home in Atlanta, I decided to take a nap and get some rest before returning to Tennessee to see my grandmother. While lying on the couch, I received a call from my aunt, yelling and screaming into the phone that my grandmother had passed away. Again, I grabbed my keys and got on the road. I spent countless hours with my father as he tried to comfort me through the unyielding storms of life I was experiencing. With the upcoming homegoing services, I believed I'd finally have a chance to breathe and begin the much-needed grieving process from all of the sudden losses I had experienced in such a short time.

While fellowshipping with my family at my grandmother's repass, I received the call that I was needed back on a mission to combat a deadly virus that had impacted the human population on a global level and to prepare my family as the nation was about to go into a lockdown in the upcoming days. As an Emergency Disaster Response nurse, I was concerned, but I immediately followed orders as I always did and prepared my home and my family for this unknown threat. A week later, I found myself isolated in a hotel room as I braved the frontlines taking care of Covid positive patients. Life as I knew it had abruptly changed, and the world was in a crisis.

Imagine experiencing so much loss and then having to isolate yourself from all of your loved ones because of your career. Imagine not having time to grieve because you were called upon to aid in the fight against this unknown virus while thoughtlessly jeopardizing your own life to carry out your duties. Imagine having to show up to work and being stuck in a cycle of no days off and monumental patient loss due to this deadly virus. I was still on a journey; however, I couldn't process my own life experience as I couldn't risk breaking down.

I was being counted on to physically show up for my patients, emotionally show up for my family, and spiritually show up for my purpose. Yet, I had never felt more abandoned in my entire life. While I was showing up for everyone else, I was alone with no one to show up for me. This saddened me, but there was no time to accept that as truth. I had to keep going. In the midst of it all, I had a book that was an international bestseller. I was thriving on a professional level while simultaneously broken in spirit.

Months went by, then October came, and while on vacation in Jamaica for a brief break, I wound up placing a call to my ex. He immediately answered, and we found ourselves in the middle of a long conversation about nothing. He began by saying he wanted to apologize for how things went down. Although I replied there was no need to apologize, truthfully, I was still hurt and felt I deserved the apology. That call became the beginning of us reconnecting again, ending our eight-month-long separation.

I was on assignment in New Mexico at the time, and our daily communication was welcoming. We had been communicating daily for months when he finally admitted he was still in what he called a situationship with the woman he had cheated on me with. I thanked him for being honest, but for some reason, this time, it changed nothing between us. We continued to communicate. January of 2021 came, and he experienced the loss of a close family member, his cousin, who had been like a brother to him. I was halfway across the country, but I did what I could to be there for him emotionally and covered him in prayer daily.

This continued until June 2021, when my father passed away unexpectedly. My ex had been in Hawaii celebrating his birthday and immediately reached out to me upon his return to Nashville and learning of my father's passing. He offered his condolences and made certain I was okay. He continued to be an emotional support. We even went to Jamaica together a few months later, where he experienced a medical emergency that led to me accompanying him to the hospital and staying by his side the entire night. The morning came, and the hospital staff insisted I leave the treatment area and wait up front to prevent unnecessary exposure to anything. I complied.

Upon separating us, my ex refused treatment and was soon discharged. He called for a taxi to take us back to the resort. We both climbed into the backseat of the car when he placed his hand on my knee and kept it there as a measure of comfort after such an ordeal. By this time, we had become accustomed to being a source of support in each other's life. We celebrated each other's accomplishments, such as when he was commissioned as a fire marshal, and with each milestone I hit in business and my career. Our connection was easy. We spent that night making love to the sounds of throwback R&B.

A few weeks later, I was thrown a curveball when I attended my sister LaToya's annual Halloween party. To my surprise, I found myself face-to-face with him and the other woman in the same room. My heart dropped knowing we had just returned from our trip to the islands, and there he was, escorting the woman who had been a root subject at the end of our relationship to a gathering at my sister's home. So many emotions ran through me. Should I expose him and cause her the same pain I had experienced just a year and a half prior as she stood arrogantly exposing him to me, telling me that she knew about me all along and still chose to start a sexual relationship with him? Or should I just let it be? After all, it wasn't my character to inflict intentional pain on another, regardless of the pain they had caused me.

I was better than that, so I pleasantly greeted the two of them and kept it moving. I struggled with the decision not to expose the truth that night because didn't she deserve the same anguish of having to stand there as another woman gloated about being with her man? Did she not deserve to go to bed crying night after night with no answers? Why had he not been so careless with her heart? Did she not deserve to live the truth that she so willingly participated in when she decided to be a part of my life? In the end, I decided she didn't deserve that. No woman does.

The next morning, I received a call from him apologizing for putting me in that position the night before. He asked if he could come to see me at my aunt's house that night before I left town. When he showed up, we talked for a while and ended up making out in his truck. There was something in me that wouldn't say no to him even when I should have, and our encounters continued that way.

The following Spring, we found ourselves in Breckenridge, Colorado, staying the night together during a group ski trip. He held me all night long. Over the next few months, we grew closer. When my birthday rolled around in July, he woke me up to a "Send me your Cash App" call and well wishes for my day. I was very appreciative and reminded of all the reasons why I fell in love with him. It was his attention to detail. I continued to see him until my trip to Dubai in October 2022.

The passing of my father had been crippling for me. My father was my soul mate. We were one and the same. He was my loudest cheerleader, counselor, comforter, listening ear, rider, warrior, and protector. The first time I experienced great loss, I was isolated by external circumstances. When I experienced the loss of my father, I isolated myself due to unprocessed internal pain. My father had been the one to try to help me navigate my breakup with my ex, and now here, my ex was trying to help me navigate the loss of my father. Both were aware of how much the other meant to me, and both played a role in trying to soften the impact of the pain.

I left for Dubai with the intent to leave all my unresolved pain across the waters. I had long known I needed to make some changes and honor my boundaries. I was done with running, comprising, and masking the pain. While on my trip, I had an experience with God where I asked him to remove anything blocking me from the blessings he had for me and to cover me.

Spending some time in the Arabian desert, I felt so close to God that it was as if he had physically manifested next to me. That day felt like a spiritual cleansing. I cried and took time to finally grieve my grandmother, best friend, father, and, most importantly, my relationship with my ex. Although we were actively seeing each other, I knew it was time to let him go. I left Dubai feeling renewed.

As I was boarding my flight back, a random stranger asked me if I believed in God-led encounters, to which I replied that I did. No further conversation was had, and that struck me as odd. The remainder of the flight back was uneventful. Once we were back on American soil and walking through customs, I was approached by a man who had been standing behind me in line. He had been sitting only two rows in front of me on my flight back. He opened the conversation by complimenting me on the sneakers I wore. We ended up having a three-hour-long conversation at the airport, which eventually led to a new romantic connection—the first with someone other than my ex since our original split in 2020.

I returned home faced with the decision to continue in a situation I knew no longer served me in the manner I deserved or to take a chance on someone new. I decided to move forward in faith. I cut ties with my ex and walked into a new season. As I got to know the man who had captured my heart in the middle of John F Kennedy Airport, I came to learn that he was an extremely accomplished composer, engineer, producer, and songwriter who is responsible for some of our beloved top-charting R&B hits from the '90s through present day. Also, he and his former partner were responsible for one of the longest-running ad jingles ever made, forever changing how commercial advertising is done.

Initially, I recall wondering how I could be so favored. This little girl who had lived such a trauma-filled life and had been beaten up so much by the journey. I didn't feel like I deserved a man such as him until one day, in conversation with a good friend Shanay, she posed the question, "Why not you?" Immediately, I knew that was God sending confirmation of his promise through her. I had spent so much time suppressing my experiences that trauma had become somewhat normalized to me. It wasn't until I went to God, lying all my burdens at his feet and crying out for his guidance, that things changed for me.

I love and experience life from a healthy place now. I embrace all aspects of life without fear now. I have lived, loved, and lost. Finding love and peace within is not a destination but rather a journey that begins the second you're born and continues until your last breath. As long as you live, life will present you with opportunities to choose love and to choose peace. It's better to make that choice proactive than reactive; live in the truth that traumas will come, but so will God's promises for your life. Make the choice that will serve you well.

This brings us full circle to our original point of who you will decide to be. Wherever you choose to journey in life, I pray you choose the road that requires you to travel through an atmosphere of healing where you will develop the character to always choose love clothed in peace, much as I had done and continue to do. When given the opportunity to hurt the other woman, I didn't. When given the opportunity to hurt my ex, I didn't. I repeatedly chose love and peace even in the midst of my own pain, and God has restored my heart and spirit while returning to me more than tenfold what I had lost, and he will do the same for you. Keep pushing. God has you.

BIO

Princess Faith

Princess Faith is breaking down barriers for BIPOC in the entertainment industry. Founder of Harper Mills, a full-service entertainment group located in Los Angeles, California, she has made it her life work to change the narrative not only for herself and her children but for families whose dynamics were similar to hers. Princess Faith has traveled the world speaking on large platforms and spreading awareness of how branding is the tool she used to change her life. Some of her brands are Kinky Kouture, The Reel Kinky Krew, Vaug – Dor, and The Intimate Dr. Princess Faith can be found on IG: TheRealKinkyPrincess or website Princess.Faith

COMING FROM BEHIND THE BUSH

TE TRICE

COMING FROM BEHIND THE BUSH

Peek A Boo.... I see you. You see who? I know you do not see me. I'm that Black Bitch as my father called me once upon a time in my younger years. In my mind, that is all he saw, and that is all of who I thought I was. Nothing more than a Black BITCH! Hearing those words come out of my father's mouth was hurtful enough, but not knowing why was just as bad. Fear was already the primary force in my life. Add to that self-hate, and you got war and confusion within. Dear God, why me? Why am I here? Why does my daddy not love me? Why would my daddy say such a horrible thing to his own daughter? Why God, why?

For years I would repeatedly ask God those questions in my thoughts and prayers. Many nights teardrops would roll down my face and onto my pillow because I never got an answer from Him. At least I did not think I had. God has a way and a timing to teach you all that you need, but only when you allow yourself to be open to receive it.

For a long time, without realizing what was happening, I didn't like looking at myself in the mirror. Over and over, all I could hear were those words coming out of my father's mouth. In those days, people in my area didn't know anything about anxiety or depression, and if they did, it was nothing that was spoken about publicly. It was obvious when someone was not quite right or if someone you knew was not acting the same. Yet we lived day by day as if everything were good, when honestly, it was not. What went on in the home stayed in the home. You did not dare go and tell anyone anything about what was happening. I tried to ask my mother questions, but she had no answers, for my mother was dealing with her own abuse. Each day it would take all her strength to push through. After all, she had me and my brother to take care of as well.

I never had insecurities about who I was until I started questioning why I had to be born black. Many times, I would go into the bathroom and ask myself, "Why are you here? Why were you born? Why were you born black? Who are you? What's the point of being here when I don't like who I see in the mirror?" Those words that danced in my head for such a long time played a big part in my depression and hatred toward myself because I had no answers.

Going into junior high and throughout my high school years, I found myself wanting to change. I did not like my hair anymore. I started playing around with makeup and using skin brighteners to change my brown skin tone because I had such a negative image playing in my head of being called Black BITCH. I no longer wanted to be black. Why was I not born white? Why couldn't I have been born with my mother's skin tone? Why did I have to be born with my father's skin tone? I do not like who I am!

Looking back, I realize that I really didn't know what I was thinking at the time because I had yet to find out exactly who I was. Think about it; I was just a young inexperienced teenager living in a household where it was very physically, mentally, and emotionally abusive for me, my mother, and my youngest brother. Each of us lived in our own little world with no one to talk to regarding our troubles. Like many kids, our escape was extracurricular activities such as sports, music, and work if we were of age.

I obtained my first job at 15, and it, along with sports, was my escape. My mom was my biggest fan and supporter. She may not have come to all of my softball and basketball games, but she came when she could. As for my dad, he worked. I cannot recall seeing him at any of my events except my middle school and high school graduation. He was there in attendance, along with my mother and brother.

Growing up in my home, we did not engage in family conversations. Life plans and future outlooks were not taught there. I grew up in survival mode. I do not remember having a happy life as a little girl. Though I did exist, I was hidden, not seen. I did not know how to be a little girl. My life was more of a fight-or-flight life, not living but surviving to make it another day. I grew up more like a "tomboy." What I was taught growing up was how to grow food, how to fish, how to hunt, how to cook, how to load and shoot a gun, and how to go to work every day. So yes, I know how to survive.

I was fun to be around, loved to smile, loved to listen to music, loved to dance, loved to sing, and loved sports, but I did not like who I was and did not know who or what was to become of my life. I wanted to be seen and heard but did not know how to begin. Life became robotic for me. I lived and behaved by routine. I had to live one way at home, but I could breathe and relax just a little when I was at school. This cycle continued for years.

I remember it like it was yesterday when my dad got hurt on the job. He worked for the railroad for some time until injury struck. I could see the fear in my moms' eyes and the sound in her voice. Dad was the breadwinner in the home, and with him being injured and about to have back surgery, what was going to happen? Recovery time was long and hard for my dad, and it was rough for my mom having to take care of him. Having to depend on my mom to do it all was not my dad's cup of tea. It seems he became meaner. He could not move, drink, smoke, or even wash himself; however, he could still use his mouth, so the verbal abuse continued. Despite all this, my mom was right there by his side.

Months had passed, and my dad was up and walking after major back surgery. He seemed calmer, but don't worry; it did not last long! I remember my dad calling me into the living room and showing me a check. I stuttered, reading the amount of money the check was written for. Holy shit! We are moving up like the Jeffersons! I had never seen a six-figured check written out before. Wow, what a relief! No more worries about money.

Soon after, Dad moved us into a white neighborhood. We were the third family of color to move there. To this day, no other families of color live in the neighborhood. Dad was able to pay cash for our family home. Cars, satellite dishes (never had cable before), fully furnished, bigger bedrooms, a dog, a pool, a patio, and plenty of food, all sitting on two acres of land. Talk about the good life! Life was good for a moment, and then the abuse started again. Dad was not used to having money like that. Money was always paycheck to paycheck. Now he had more than ever before, and he made sure you knew he had it and the money was his.

After graduating high school at the age of 17, I thought living would get easier. It seems as though it got worse. You would think having that freedom would bring about a certain peace, but it did not. I knew it was time to find my way, yet before I could do so, more difficulties found their way to me. Still full of hurt, anger, and confusion, I felt as though the world was about to come crashing down on me. The pressures of life seemed to be unbearable. I felt like I could not take it anymore. The drinking, fighting, fear, and isolation would not go away. I found myself entertaining the thought of suicide. I felt many times I could not take it any longer. I wanted a way out! What I was going through could not be all that life had to offer.

Facing each day became more and more difficult. I would find myself stressed out to the point of shaking inside daily. I would use the bathroom as my private place to cry, stare at the mirror, and ask WHY!!!! God... Why me? Why are we living like this? That was the main question I would have on repeat. Constantly I would play in my mind how to bring this miserable way of living to an end. I thought the same thoughts that so many others have, but I could not go through with it.

After a year of contemplating on doing this and that, I packed up everything I could and left. I had an older friend I knew, and I told her what I was dealing with. She offered me a place to stay for a moment. Although I was of age, I had no clue about what I was doing other than leaving an abusive home, which led me to experience life in a whole new light! I did not admit it at the time, but I had to be going crazy! I left an all-brick ranch home with my own bedroom for a couch. I had no job, was low on money, and my car insurance was coming up. What was I to do? I had to find work.

My friend and I set out to find employment, and we did. Having a job brought about a little bit of relief. I was back saving and making plans to get my own place. About a month or so passed by, and my friend had a friend with a friend looking for a friend. Lord, why? This had to be a setup because it appeared to be all fun and freedom. It is not like I knew what I was doing anyway, so I went with the flow of it. Big mistake! I went from sugar to shit! I fell head over heels in LUST over this guy I was introduced to. I went from having a car, a place to lay my head, food, a job, and necessities to having no car, being jobless, and being homeless. Sometimes standing outside at night for hours underneath a streetlight, wishing I could just sleep. I dared not to ask the "why" question again.

This time I was full of shame and guilt for what I had allowed to happen to me. Although I was not an experienced young lady, and God knows I did not know anything about being on my own, no one should be manipulated as much as I was during the entire time I was following behind this person. I was totally taken advantage of. After about a few weeks of being homeless, there was this elderly woman that needed help with cleaning her apartment. She asked if I could help, and of course I did, but the love she had in her heart got us a room in her home in exchange for me helping her with whatever she needed me to do. Thankful is an understatement of how I felt.

Sadly, I was still following behind this jerk of a person, and after about a month or so, we ventured off to his hometown where I began living with his cousin. This home was the go-to spot on the weekends. I was shocked at everything I was seeing for the first time in my life. Anything you could imagine was taking place at his cousin's house. I was as green as they come in an environment where you really needed to be on your toes. It took a moment to get used to, but I quickly learned how to read people and watch the behavior of others in order for me to know how to move when people came around. My survival mentality was on one thousand daily, especially at night, for you never knew what could pop off.

The romance ended a few months after being brought into his cousin's home when his true self came to light. A situation happened one Saturday night, and before you knew it, I remember picking up a bottle to bust his head wide open, and it was snatched out of my hand before I made contact. He never saw it coming. I truly did not know I had that much anger inside of me; I was fed up and wanted no more bullshit from him or anyone else. I was pushed into another room, and he was taken outside to separate us, which was the best thing because that night, I was ready for whatever.

For once, I took a serious look at myself and how I was living and made up my mind that I was done and had to make a change. I ended the roller coaster he had me on and never went back with him again. I landed a job and set out to save as much money as possible while paying for my stay at the house. I was in grind mode and otherwise unavailable unless it was about a better job or transportation. Every day that I was on schedule, I got up and walked to my job, determined to get back on my feet the right way and find my own apartment. It was time to take charge. I declared, "I am coming from behind this bush, and I will have PEACE!"

Months passed, and I was still working. Thinking I had enough money to purchase a car, I started shopping around. I needed to pay cash for transportation, but nothing showed up. As I was out and about, someone who knew me approached me and said people were looking for me and that it was an emergency. I thought to myself, what in the world could be going on? I returned to the house where I was staying and called to find out what was happening. They told me I needed to get to the hospital immediately because my mom had been admitted. Oh my God! My heart began to race as my mind went to the worst scenario.

What was I going to do? Not giving a damn about anybody else's feelings, I knew I needed to get to my mom.

I started my search for a ride to get me to the hospital. It took me two days! Anxiously, I arrived at the hospital not knowing what to expect. I got to my mom's room, and I broke down crying. Sitting in the chair was my dad, whom I was not ready to see; however, I was not going to let that interfere with me being there for my mother. The pain in my heart for my mom came crashing down at that very moment. I sat there with her all day.

I was able to speak with the nurse and doctor to find out what was going on. How in the world was my mom still alive? She needed a blood transfusion and had to undergo bone marrow surgery. At this point, I had to get things in order to be with my mom through all of this. As I was preparing to leave and come back the next day, my dad blocked the door so I could not go. I was so full of rage!

I did not know what to do. I had no phone or transportation. Here my mom was lying in a hospital bed, and my dad pulled this stunt! Words cannot express the type of emotion I was feeling. You name it, I either felt that way or thought it. I held back the tears so my mom could remain comfortable. With fear settling back in, I opted to stay in the hospital with my mom so I did not have to ride home with my dad. A few days passed, and all went well with the procedures, and Mom went home. Thank you, God, for keeping my mother!

Soon after being forced to come back home, I was able to purchase a car, obtain a good job and move into my very first apartment. Just to be able to breathe and be at peace was everything to me! For once, I had a smile on my face, and I was starting to peel off those layers that had weighed me down. The journey was just beginning. Considering all that I had been through up to this point, I may have been bruised, but I did not break, which meant that I would heal. I decided to keep on going and see what was next.

After about a year of working and living on my own, the opportunity presented itself for me to make a move. My mind was made up, and I felt an overwhelming push to take the leap and go. I rented a U-Haul truck, packed all that I had, and struck out with my brother and a family friend in the middle of a snowstorm with ice expected to arrive. The streets were clear when we left, so we thought we would beat the ice before it accumulated. How about we got stuck on the interstate for hours due to bad weather! There we were stuck with no food or water, just boxes of clothing. I swear I cannot win for losing!

We had been stuck on the interstate for so long that all three of us sat there sleeping inside the truck. It was midday when we each began to wake up. Traffic was still not moving. My brother was becoming anxious and decided to get out of the truck and start walking to see if he could find out some information from anyone. During this time, we did not have cell phones. All we had was a mouth and a prayer. I used both. I would be willing to bet that my brother and our family friend did too!

A few more hours had passed when traffic slowly started moving again. We were so happy! Words could not express how we felt at that time. Moving slow as a turtle, it was stop and go, stop and go, until we suddenly stopped again. As we sat there, I began to pray. Tired, hungry, and full of frustration, I asked God how much longer. Instantly the truck started moving. Mind you, the truck was in park, but for whatever reason, the truck started sliding. We were on ice!

Talk about fear. To the right of us was a cliff with no guard rails, just straight down. The truck continued moving toward the right. When I tell you, I yelled out to God with

74

all the authority I had in me. "GOD, NO! WE NEED YOUR STRENGTH NOW, GOD!" Right before the truck was to go over the cliff, it stopped and literally slid back to the left, all while being in park. Tears began to roll down my face, and it was then that I saw the Power of God take control over a situation I had no control over. Whatever this thing called life is, it can be confusing, scary at times, and downright frustrating; however, I'm still here. And God was not done with me yet!

Time passed, and I was working, saving money, living in a nice apartment, and finally relaxing. I spoke to Mom weekly to see how she was doing and to make sure she did all the doctors told her to do based on her health. Occasionally, Dad would get on the phone to speak and see how I was doing. After a very long time, it actually started feeling good to hear my dad's voice. Healing had not quite begun, but there was peace just being able to inhale and exhale in my own space. Giving myself grace just to be me was so needed in my life at that time and still is to this day.

Every so often, I would go home on the weekends to visit. The first few times weren't easy because I was still uncomfortable visiting home. After all, that was where my traumatic experiences happened; nevertheless, I would go because of my love for my mom, dad, and youngest brother. Sundays couldn't come fast enough to leave and return to my own space. I was still discovering who I was and needing my own peace while learning how to love myself.

I can remember when Mom and Dad came to visit me one weekend. There was a smile on my face because, deep down inside, I was still a daddy's girl needing her father. I was an adult, and I still needed my father. I can recall a time when I heard a sermon being spoken about the power of forgiveness. I really didn't understand that forgiveness was not for the other person but for your own healing. At that point, I knew I had to forgive my dad for the things that I was put through because he didn't know any better, and I had to forgive my mom as well. I also needed to forgive myself, but at the time, I had not. I thought more about the forgiveness I needed to give versus the forgiveness I needed for myself. After the sermon and after studying scripture and understanding more, I realized I needed to let things go and find love in my heart again for my father because there was such brokenness and distance within our family. I forgave and started trying to find myself even more so than what I was doing before that particular sermon.

A couple of years later, I was on my way home for the Christmas holiday. On Christmas Eve, I was in the kitchen as usual, helping my mom prepare the Christmas meal by chopping up vegetables, washing turnip greens, peeling sweet potatoes, and listening to music. We were laughing and talking, and Mom had the turkey in the oven. You could smell the aroma throughout the air. I actually had a smile on my face. All in all, I felt comfortable, and it was good.

Christmas came, and we all sat around, ate dinner, exchanged gifts, and visited other family members; it was a long, happy day. We came home, rested, then ate again. A couple of days passed, and I was out visiting old friends I hadn't seen in a while, hanging out with them catching up on old times, then visiting people I used to work with at my old job, and just relaxing for a change. It was nice being at home in my old room. December 28th came around, and I was at the gas station gassing up my car. I was going to visit a couple more friends I hadn't seen. I told them I would come by before I got ready to leave and go back because I had to get back to work.

For some strange reason, my dad drove up to the gas station where I was gassing up the car to ask me if I was leaving that night. I told him no, I was just putting gas in the car and planned to leave out in the morning, which would have been December 29th, my dad's birthday. He had this concern in his voice and a look in his eyes that I'll never forget as he told me to be careful and not to be out late and get back home safely. I told him no problem. I was just going to visit a couple of friends and then come in because I had to get ready to leave that next morning. So, I left and went to visit a few people, but while I was driving, the Spirit of God spoke to me as clearly as if it was someone in the car with me and said I need you to pray for your dad as you do for your mother. I was not confused about what I heard but puzzled as to why.

I came home, finished packing up all my stuff, loaded up my car, and went to bed expecting to get up in the morning so I could get ready to head out. That didn't happen. On December 29th, I was in my room sleeping when I heard a loud noise hit the floor. I heard the screams of my mother calling for me. I jumped up and raced to the kitchen to find my father lying on the floor. Immediately I began CPR. While the ambulance was on its way, my dad became unresponsive. I kept calling his name and asking him to squeeze my hands if he could hear me. His eyes were rolling in the back of his head, and a gurgling noise came from his breath.

My dad died in my arms on December 29th, his birthday. I never got to wish my father a happy birthday or to tell him I loved him. Thankfully, two years prior, my dad and I had made peace with one another. I am so grateful to God that I had the opportunity to find peace with my father. Looking back on all that I have gone through tells me I'm built for this journey. The strength of many is carrying me through, and for that, I am blessed.

BIO

TE TRICE

She is called Ms. Te. Ms. Te is an experienced female entrepreneur in Nashville, TN. She had no clue what it would take to have a business but was determined to have one. Ms. Te has worked as an entrepreneur for eight years since leaving a very toxic corporate career.

Always creative in her thoughts toward business, Ms. Te found a passion for helping others. She knows how important it is to have self-confidence when starting a business from beginning to end and has invested in being of service to others.

Initially, she was educated by taking nursing courses. This was not her goal but her father's wishes, so that journey began and ended quickly. Ms. Te later obtained her AAS degree from a local junior college. This started a long career in the medical and health industry. Later in life, she found herself living as a single mom and needed to find a way to bring in more money.

Years later, Ms. Te graduated with a Business and Organizational Development degree from Bethel University. With that accomplishment came an opportunity she had never dreamed of. She was offered a college instructor adjunct Professor position at a local college with no experience, just years of skills. Never think you can't do something! Fast forward to 2023, after years of delay, she launched her new business called Tranquility Homes, LLC in March. This is business number two.

Ms. Te loves spending time with her family, baking, cooking, and traveling in her spare time. Currently living in Nashville, she enjoys the diversity of the city.

If you'd like to get in contact with Te, send an email to thllc2002@gmail.com

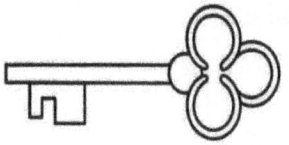

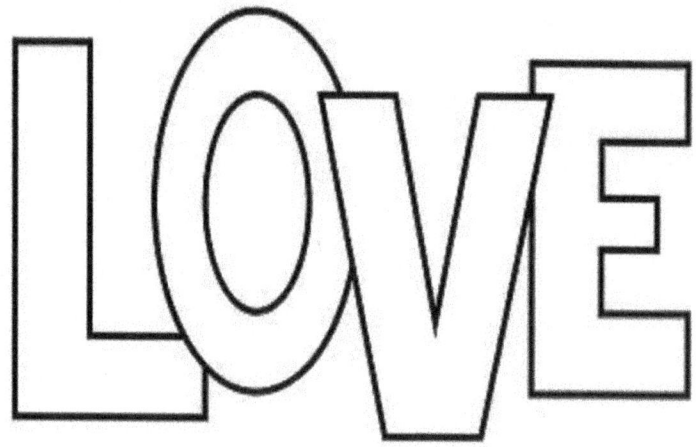

Finding Love and
Peace Within.

IT'S NEVER TOO LATE TO FIND LOVE & PEACE

ANGELA LEWIS

DEDICATION

I dedicate this chapter to my husband, Dewayne.

What seemed like the worst move turned out to be the best move.

It's only up from here!

I Love You!!!

IT'S NEVER TOO LATE TO FIND LOVE & PEACE

"Do not be anxious about anything, but in everything by prayer and supplication with thanksgiving let your requests be made known to God. And the peace of God, which surpasses all understanding, will guard your hearts and your minds in Christ Jesus." Philippians 4:6-7

They say everything you need is already inside you, so finding love and peace within shouldn't be hard to do, right? Unfortunately, that isn't always the case. Many people struggle with low self-esteem, self-worth issues, and expressing self-love. Oftentimes we look outside of ourselves to find love and peace rather than doing the work to find love and peace within. Society plays a huge role by constantly bombarding us with the latest shiny object that is a must-have or telling us we need the perfect house, perfect car, perfect job, perfect man (woman), or we need to look a certain way to be accepted. Sadly, none of the "perfect" things matter when you are dissatisfied with who you are.

When did we stop feeling good enough? When did we stop living and just start existing? What happened that took away our joy, peace, passion, and zest for life? Some of us have experienced so much trauma and drama in our lives that it became too much to do anything more than be a functioning adult. Sure, we smiled at the appropriate times or laughed on cue, but our hearts weren't really in it. We went about life behaving as if everything was fine, but deep down, we had checked out and detached from everything around us.

How can you not be anxious about anything and find love and peace within when your heart has been broken and you have built an impenetrable wall that no one can get past to hurt you ever again? You have withdrawn to a safe space and gotten comfortable. You hide behind a mask, refusing to allow the real you to show up. I've been there and done that! And it was exhausting.

How many of you know the biggest lie you can tell is the one that you tell yourself? If you can't be honest with yourself, who can you be honest with? The answer is God. See, you aren't fooling God because he already knows everything about you. Jeremiah 1:5 says, *"I knew you before I formed you in your mother's womb. Before you were born I set you apart and appointed you."* Luke 12:7 says, *"But even the very hairs of your head are all numbered."* The Bible will drop some powerful truths on you. You have to decide if you are ready to hear them.

From the outside looking in, my life seemed good. I was married, had two kids, was running a business, had great friends, and things seemed perfect. I was part of a women's organization, and we had a trip planned for Cancun in August 2022. I was all ready for some fun in the sun with my girls. I celebrated my 55th birthday with a big party in April and was still in celebration mode as we boarded the plane. We got to Mexico, checked into the resort, and proceeded to have a phenomenal time. All you could eat and drink and lots of poolside fun.

Things at home weren't bad, but they weren't necessarily good either. I told myself that I would enjoy this break and when I got back, I would do better and get out of the rut I had been in for a while. I had been saying that 2023 would be my Jordan Year, and I was ready for something different. Little did I know how different it would be.

On the flight home, I was thinking about the conversation I planned on having with my husband. Our anniversary was coming up on September 2nd, so I thought it would be good to clear the air and start making plans for our best year ever. When I got home, it was quiet, but I didn't think anything about it. I unpacked, turned on the tv, and decided to binge-watch until my husband got home.

It was getting late, and I got out my cell phone to check and make sure he was okay since it was past the time that he would normally be there. I texted him earlier, letting him know I was home, but I never received a response. I dialed the numbers, and he answered, but the conversation was not what I expected. He said he was okay but wasn't planning on coming home. He had been thinking about some things himself and needed time alone.

I looked at the phone like, WHAT? What do you mean you need some time alone? Instead of saying those words, I chose to be hard and just said, "Oh, okay." In my head, I thought he was being petty because I had been out of the country. We got off the phone, and I looked around with fresh eyes and noticed a few things were missing. In disbelief, I realized he had left for real.

Sometimes God gives you whispers and allows you to address issues before they become too big. I wish I had paid attention then, but I did things my way. I didn't want to see what was right in front of me, so I stayed behind the big wall I had created and became more and more detached as the years went by. What could have been easily fixed years ago turned into the one thing I had been protecting myself from - losing someone else I loved.

I have experienced a lot of loss over the years. My parents and grandparents were deceased, along with two sisters, my stepson, ex-husband, aunts, uncles, cousins, and good friends. It just felt like grief was always around the corner. I always felt like I had to be strong, and it was really rare for me to cry. I bottled all of those emotions up and did everything I could not to release them. Yet, this hit a little differently.

I was divorced before, so I guess, in some ways, I was waiting for this marriage to end the same way. But this time, I was caught off guard because I thought I had time to get things back on track. I had thought about what I would say while chilling on the beach or relaxing in the pool in Mexico. I felt in my spirit that we could turn things around, and 2023 would be our best year ever! The sad thing was I waited too late, and I had no one to blame but myself.

Dealing with a separation is hard, but I knew I had to take responsibility for my actions that got us there. I couldn't blame my husband for everything. I had to look at the person in the mirror and work on me. I asked God to help me be a better me, and if my marriage could be saved, then great; if not, I would have to accept that outcome too. It was then that I took a good look at what it meant to be a woman empowered.

I had a Facebook group called I Am a Woman Empowered that was started in 2020, but just like my life, I had let it run on autopilot, doing the bare minimum to keep it going. That was not what it meant to be empowered. I decided it was time for me to do the work on myself. As I was working on myself, I would pour into the group, and we would become empowered together.

That is when Philippians 4:6-7 became real to me. As I petitioned God, trusted him, and worked on me, I started finding love and peace within. I wasn't blaming my husband. I wasn't begging and pleading. I went back to the basics and began re-developing my relationship with God and putting him first. I started praying and fasting and putting myself first. I was working on me as I asked God to work on my husband. I began to break down the walls that I had built up and released emotions that had been backed up for years. I started to feel free and at peace, anxious for nothing.

Slowly, my husband and I started having conversations. We communicated differently and talked about where we were going and our visions and goals. We began to see each other more clearly, and we weren't taking each other for granted. He noticed the changes I was making, and I saw the efforts he was putting in. We didn't rush it but took the time to become strong separately before becoming strong together. As I look back, it was the decision to take my life back and become empowered that allowed me to find love and peace within. I hope this blueprint will help you on your journey to finding the love and peace within you.

EMPOWER

E: **Stop making excuses.** I had to honestly assess my situation and stop making excuses for it. I was where I was because of the poor choices and decisions I made. Once I stopped making excuses and became accountable, I started getting different results.

M: **Manifest the right mindset.** I had to switch from a poverty mindset to an abundance mindset and manifest the things I wanted to see in my life. A poverty mindset is not always about finances. You can operate in a poverty mindset when you let things slide that need to be addressed or put off something important for something non-essential.

I began to speak life to myself and my situation through daily affirmations. I started to give things over to God to keep my peace, and I chose not to worry about how things looked and focused solely on God and me.

P: Prayed until I had Peace. There's something about giving things to God in prayer and trusting Him to put His Super over your natural that gives you peace. That's that peace that surpasses ALL understanding. As I was pursuing God, I trusted the process. I released any expectations of the outcome, knowing that all things work together for my good. So, I prayed not my will but God's will be done and asked that He give me the grace to accept whatever the outcome.

O: Owned My Shit. YES! I had to take ownership of the part I played in the mess I made—point blank, period!

W: Work. That's it, that's all. I had to put in the work on myself to come out victorious on the other side. Faith without works is dead.

E: Stayed Encouraged. I didn't give up on my marriage. What God has for me is for me, and I had to believe in that wholeheartedly, regardless of what it looked like. Sometimes we have to stop asking other people to pray for us, telling them all of our business, and getting their opinions. Sometimes, we have to encourage ourselves while we are going through. Everything you need is already inside of you, as I stated in the beginning. Edify and encourage yourself and watch miracles happen.

R: Remember Who I Am. I had to remember that I am a child of God, and I am fearfully and wonderfully made. I had to respect myself and stop entertaining mediocrity. It was time for me to rise up and be the Queen God created me to be. I had to remind myself that I had a life that was worth living, married or single, and I could not make my husband see me higher than I saw myself. Once I remembered who I was, the game changed.

~~~~~~

I hope you will take the time to EMPOWER yourself and use these nuggets to find the love and peace within YOU! Life is a precious gift, and we were not meant to be mediocre and play small. We were meant to SHINE and be a light to the world. When I shine, you shine, we shine together, and together we can light up the whole world!!!

BIO

ANGELA LEWIS

Voted one of the "Top 50 Empowered Women Empowering Women" by *Called2Inspire Magazine*, empowerment expert Angela Lewis is a highly sought-after international keynoter, bestselling author, and visibility coach. Highly regarded as one of the most influential voices of motivational speaking, Angela is now on a mission to impact audiences and train individuals and corporations worldwide with her message of encouragement and empowerment, so they reach their highest potential.

Angela's extensive expertise had earned her invitations to speak on major stages across the country. She has delivered dynamic live and virtual keynote speeches for large audiences, including Shawn Fair's Leadership Experience Tour, Queens Roundtable Symposium, and Sister Leader Conference, to name a few.

She is a compelling thought leader and motivational speaker dedicated to supporting women's personal and professional empowerment worldwide. In line with her unyielding passion for helping others succeed, Angela founded "Hot Wife Society" and "I Am a Woman Empowered," initiatives that provide women opportunities to build confidence, connections, and collaborations through workshops, conferences, personal consultations, and entrepreneurial ventures.

Angela has a deep-rooted enthusiasm for helping women use their gifts, talents, and voice. She mentors passionately, guiding her clients with results-proven strategies that provide the visibility and credibility needed for their brands to "elevate and dominate" in the marketplace. She founded

A & M Publishing & Productions, a company that has assisted thousands of women in publishing literary works. She is the visionary of two bestselling book anthologies; *I Am a Woman Empowered: Stories of Strength, Resiliency & Triumphs*, and *Woman Empowered 2: Fierce, Fabulous & Free*. These books give women the voice to share their personal stories to empower others.

Angela is an inspirational figure and has been recognized for her leadership, dedication, and contributions to her community and the next generation. Her work has been featured on prominent media platforms such as *Own It! Magazine, SwagHer Magazine, Tap-In Magazine, Pretty Women, Hustle Online*, talk shows, podcasts, newspapers, and more.

Email: info@iamangelalewis.com
Website: https://www.iamangelalewis.com
LinkedIn: https://www.linkedin.com/in/angela-lewis-6b5243141
Instagram: https://www.instagram.com/iamangelalewis
Facebook: https://www.facebook.com/100000056166247
Twitter: https://twitter.com/_iamangelalewis

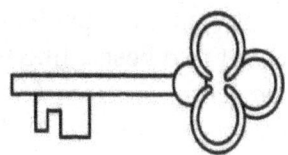

COOL2BKIDS.COM

Finding Love and

Peace Within.

HEAVILY HEALED
Freda Stevenson

"But by the grace of God, I am what I am: and his grace which was bestowed upon me was not in vain; but I labored more abundantly than they all: yet not I, but the grace of God which was with me." (1 Corinthians 15: 10)

Dedication

I dedicate my chapter to any woman who feels unworthy, uncertain, lonely, and unloved. I feel like we as a society think everyone should be successful right away as young adults. However, everyone's success is measured differently and occurs in our lives at different times. Our personal growth should be our overall goal and should be recognized by those who see and value us.

When I think of recognition, I think of my son. I appreciate his support, motivation, and encouragement; he has been my uplifting gift since 1998. He keeps me encouraged and pushes me to achieve GREATNESS.

I am the granddaughter of the late Reverend Robert Samuel Stevenson and First Lady Wilhelmenia Fort Stevenson. I dedicate this chapter to them for teaching and helping me to become the woman I am today. They raised me to be and do my BEST despite the difficulties and

challenges surrounding me.

Freda Stevenson

Introduction

It is an honor to have the opportunity to be a part of a visionary project to help inspire and promote self-confidence and self-care. It is a blessing to encourage women who feel a sense of unworthiness due to the hardships of life.

I was a sheltered young country girl born and raised on my family's farm in Cedar Hill, TN. My maternal grandparents raised me. They loved, nurtured, and taught me everything I needed to know as I grew up to become the person I am today. I referred to them as "Mama" and "Daddy." They had already raised their six children but took it upon themselves to take me, my brother, and my cousins in as well. They ensured we went to school every day and learned to be responsible by working on the farm. They also made sure we went to church every Sunday. My grandfather was a pastor of a local church in the community.

He was an exceptional man who made sure that we were well taken care of no matter what situation he faced with a house full of children and grandchildren. We did not have much monetarily and materialistically; however, we had a small home filled with love, laughter, and, of course, chaos too. My grandparents gave me so much love and attention, and I cherish them to this day because they were the only individuals at that time that made me feel worthy.

I was not raised by either my mother or father. My mother was around me growing up and often helped her parents (my grandparents) take care of me, but it wasn't the same. My parents had me at age 19, so I often looked at my mother as an older sibling, especially with her being around only on the weekends. My mother went off to college, started her career, and created a lifestyle that was suitable to her and, from my perspective, did not involve her children.

My father was non-existent. No one informed me about him, and for years, I had no clue who or where he was nor what he looked like. Around the age of 6, I remember visiting my mother and aunt, who lived in an apartment complex in East Nashville at the time. I remember being outside helping bring in groceries with my aunt and mother, and a random man approached me and asked how I was and just stood there kind of awkwardly. I recall my mother walking up, and the man stated, "Is this your daughter? She sure has grown." I remember the awkward energy both my mother and aunt had toward this man and the man himself, carrying that same energy. Fast forward to years later, I learned that man was my father. Growing up, I had no clue what he looked like, nor had I been introduced to him. Meanwhile, he was right in front of me, and everyone shielded me from the truth instead of facing their own realities. Sad, right?

I had a good life at home with my grandparents on the farm, but I did not grow up like most regular people. Typically, young people my age get the opportunity to do fun things such as playing sports, skating, going to the park, movies, boys, etc. However, that was not my life! I worked in the fields planting and cutting tobacco, gardening, and tending to the needs of the farm.

As an adult, it still puzzles me why two people would bring a baby into the world and not raise their child. Why bring a child into the world only to abandon it at birth? I have always felt it is important to raise your own children, especially if you went through the process of creating them. It was hard enough going through life not getting the chance to experience true childhood because of working on a farm and not having the opportunity to enjoy and experience things most young people liked to do during that time. However, not having both my biological parents raise me was different and caused me to feel incomplete.

As I reflect on the past, it often makes me sad that my social skills were not addressed as they should have been growing up as a young girl. I was not talked to about the change of life for a woman. Sex and boys were not discussed in our household at all! Honestly, I did not feel comfortable asking questions because of the negative responses I would receive. It was instilled into me that we were too young to have boyfriends. I was told not to have sex until I got married, and phrases like "keep your legs closed."

As an adult, I often think about how I was discarded and essentially set up for failure at a young age. Topics such as these should never be taken lightly. Children of a certain age should be made aware of the consequences that can occur when they make the wrong choices. As a result, I lived most of my teenage years afraid to understand and experience things most girls my age were already aware of.

I became an emotional eater around the age of 10 during the mid-1970s, which was around the time my mother met and started dating my stepfather. I remember feeling very unsettled about my stepfather as a child. I always knew he was not the right fit for my mother. Number one, he was heavy-handed when it came to alcoholic beverages, which allowed me to see a different side of him.

He barely attempted to develop a relationship with me, nor did my mother insist that he should. He often made fun of my weight and constantly found a way to remind me I was not worthy because of my size. Frequently he would make statements about my eating and my weight in front of my mother, saying, "Oh, so you're eating again," or "Didn't you just eat not too long ago?"

I would often express my concerns to my mother about how I felt. She would either make excuses for him by stating, "He was joking, don't pay it no mind," or say little to nothing in my defense. I know my mother was aware that I felt uncomfortable around him because a mother knows their child. Also, my mother experienced being heavy when she was younger, so it wasn't hard to understand how I felt being treated differently because of my size.

Keep in mind I already felt unseen and neglected by my mother's inconsistent relationship with me, on top of being raised in the country and made to believe phrases like, "what happens in this house stays in this house," from the mindset of my grandparents. As a child, it gave me hope to dream about when my mother would pick me and my brother up and take us with her to live. Essentially, I wondered when she would finally decide to raise her own children. So, when my stepfather came along and was not accepting of me, and neither I nor my brother were included in the "plan" of a blended family, it created a deeper feeling of neglect.

It seemed like everything and everyone around me was dysfunctional. Sadly, I was raised not to have a voice and be okay with everyone else's dysfunction. The only thing that seemed accessible and comforting to me at that time was food.

My mother once asked for my opinion of my stepfather and their relationship before they decided to marry in the late 70s. I replied honestly based on my personal experience of him and his actions towards me and even my mother. Of course, she became defensive and made the statement, "It really didn't matter anyway because she was going to be happy." Her response to this statement illustrated that she was more focused on her image, and it clearly did not involve me or my feelings. The whole experience, along with not having a clue about my father, left me longing for love and validation.

At 18 and throughout my 20s, I can recall being involved in two serious relationships that illustrated what love was from a romantic aspect. The first relationship was when I went off to college. I met a man who was sixteen years my senior. Yes, this is when I lost my virginity. He treated me like a queen and showered me with love and materialistic things. His actions often matched his words, and even to this day, I am forever thankful for that experience. I can honestly say I loved that man, although it felt awkward and uncomfortable dating someone 16 years older than me at the time. We eventually parted ways but remained friends until he passed away.

In the early 90s, I was introduced to a close friend/co-worker's son. This man was eight years younger and full of fun, energy, love, trouble, and life—just the right amount of toxicity for a young girl during that era, lol. We became best friends and inseparable. He was my second true love like no other. At the time, I could not imagine spending the rest of my life without this man until he got heavily involved in drugs. I remember going into those dark, crack houses and areas, trying to "save" him and create a better way of life for him. Looking back, I realize you cannot change anyone, and you certainly cannot help someone who does not want to change for themselves and those around them.

I often think about the "what if's" involving that relationship, especially after his death. I can honestly say I loved this man more than I have ever loved any man. He always showed me respect and unconditional love despite not having both qualities for himself. Like most people, he was dealing with his own trauma, and after a while, I knew that was a lifestyle I was unwilling to condone or take on. God truly knew best.

It was in the mid-90s when I met my child's father. I had a toxic relationship with my child's father for over fifteen years. He was very controlling, manipulative, and self-absorbed, the definition of a Class A narcissist. Unfortunately, my child was born out of wedlock, just as I was. Six months into my pregnancy, I learned my child's father was married. When I found out, I was beyond devastated. I felt angry, hurt, and guilty. I confronted him, as any woman would, and of course, he denied every bit of it. He made statements such as, "I am not married; if I were married, I would have told you. I ought to know if I am married or not." For the longest, I blamed myself for not knowing about his marriage.

I learned my son's father was a womanizer, liar, and manipulator. He was not forthcoming about any of his personal dealings; therefore, I felt like the person I knew was nothing as he portrayed himself to be. I was so eager to make things work for my son and myself because I wanted so badly to have something I did not have growing up: a family unit. Although I tried to create a better lifestyle for myself and my child with his father, I now realize my lack of knowledge and self-worth equated to my child suffering the same things I encountered.

I often think about what life would have been like if self-worth and esteem had been taught to me as a young girl. I've contemplated what life would have been like in my 20s if I had been aware of what a narcissist was and what it meant and that everyone does not have your best interest at heart. I've even considered what life would have been like if I had known and been taught the importance of boundaries at an early age. It is one thing to be self-aware by knowing better and not doing better, but it is even worse growing up sheltered and not having a clue about anything at all.

In 2002, I came across a random picture of a man at my mother's house. My son was four, and I was 35 at the time. I remember asking her who the man was the first time, and she mentioned the man's name and stated he was "someone she had dated in the past." I kept coming across this same picture, however, and something in my spirit told me to inquire about this man again. When I asked about the man again, she decided to be forthcoming with the truth by stating the man pictured was my father.

At that moment, I was met with numerous emotions. I was finally relieved to know something about my father, but I was sad and angry because I wondered why he never attempted to come around or inquire about me. I was also mad that my mother had kept him a secret for 35 years. What upset me the most was that I had to suffer due to two grown adults' lack of maturity and inability to face their own realities.

As I eagerly discovered more about him, my mom and uncle started to tell me more stories about my father. Although I was grateful, I was also angry that all of my mother's siblings and my grandparents knew the truth and chose to withhold this information from me for 35 years.

Through conversation, my cousin and I discussed the situation at hand, and I informed her of my father's name. Unknown to me and my cousin, she and my father both worked at the same company in the early 2000s. I was able to get my father's contact information based on the endeavor of their conversation. When I met him and we conversed, he stated he knew where I was from day one. Looking back, that statement he made let me know everything I needed to know about him, and honestly, that statement still crushes me. I just wanted to know WHY? I was hurt that he would neglect me and was seemingly at peace about it.

At age 56, I can now say the wisdom I have attained over the years has helped me evolve. I have finally accepted that the unhealthy relationships I chose throughout my life all stem back to being neglected by my father and mother. Not having the skills to speak for myself and being emotionally abused caused me to become an emotional eater. Food felt like the only comforting thing for me during my lifetime, and it felt like the easiest way to suppress my pain.

I strive to change the mindset and limitations I used to have and placed upon myself and my worth. In my 30s, I was such an old lady. I was so self-conscious about my weight and appearance, not knowing there was beauty behind my shield. I shielded myself with clothing that was at least twice my size. I was a homebody, and you couldn't dare ask me where the popular spots were in Nashville because I honestly could not have told you.

Keep in mind I'm still human. However, I strive to be a better version of myself daily. In 2022, I took matters into my own hands and decided to get healthy and go on a weight loss journey. I have lost 40 pounds and am striving to lose more. In this chapter of my life, I have realized how carrying so much heaviness, weight-wise and in life, has caused me not to heal. As I become more aware of this journey, I have learned the importance of helping those around me. This journey is not just about me losing "weight," but also about getting rid of dead ends that have held me back from doing the assignment God has called me to do.

How have you evolved?

The experiences I acquired through my trials have helped me to push through difficult moments more now than ever. The hardships enabled me to think critically about my choices rather than making a quick reaction to the present situation. My experiences have also taught me to forgive those who have done me wrong throughout life. There is nothing I can do to fight my own battles; only God can fight them for me.

In January 2018, I was diagnosed with Relapsing Multiple Sclerosis with severe Occipital Neuralgia head pain. Additionally, I have Degenerative Joint Disease, Osteoarthritis and have had three hip replacements, plus suffering from obesity. I have endured a lot of health issues, but I still keep pushing myself to maintain a better quality of life. There are times when I am not at my best due to Multiple Sclerosis; however, I continue to encourage myself that this life is worth living! I am unable to control these specific circumstances, but every day I wake up is a blessing.

I strive to be an example for those around me in reference to having a positive outlook on life. I have learned the power of a positive mindset and attitude. Through maturing, I have learned this lifestyle/mindset is a choice. What you speak about yourself or think about yourself will remain your reality because of the limits one places upon oneself. At this point in life, there are numerous dreams and goals I am striving to achieve. Therefore, I am responsible for showing up with the right mindset and attitude toward my achievements.

Where are you today?

This new chapter in my life has taught me to surround myself with like-minded people who encourage me to be myself. In April of 2022, I joined Table Talk/W.O.P. (Women of Peace). This group has been a great support system for helping me become a better woman by opening up more and expressing my innermost feelings, which I used to hold within. This group has helped me to become more capable of facing and living in my truth. Latoya and the other ladies have encouraged me to work on my internal self. I want to be able to bless young women and be an inspiration to them. Subsequently, I have realized

I must do my part, which is to do the work within me. I feel honored when young people tell me they are inspired by the work I am doing within myself, and it has helped to motivate and hold them more accountable to do the work for themselves. I want to succeed; therefore, I want those around me to succeed and be their best!

I hope readers see this and understand I have been broken, but I choose not to let those flaws hold me back from reaching my full potential. There is so much I would like to contribute to society. I want to help children, teens, and young adults understand true self-worth and acceptance. This has been an issue in society for a long time, and for many (like me), it's a generational issue. It makes me uncomfortable to hear about anyone who has committed suicide over any issue because of not being accepted by society and not feeling worthy enough in a world filled with so much negativity. I can truly say the ladies in (W.O.P) Women of Peace are like my little sisters and have helped me do more critical thinking about my worth and how I can contribute to those around me.

What would you tell your younger self?

I would tell myself that it is alright not to please everyone. I must put my happiness first. I should seek goals that are attainable for me and my future and not what relatives and others feel I should do. My goal is to make sure that I am healthy mentally and physically so that I can reach my maximum potential to achieve whatever I need for my career and health. My first priority is taking care of my personal needs. I cannot afford to self-sabotage myself for others.

I would also tell myself to filter the opinions of most people. Most opinions from individuals are not built from experience and wisdom. I want young people to understand the importance of wisdom and filter what is considered an opinion and constructive- criticism. In order to evolve, all people must first humble themselves and be willing to learn from others who have walked through personal challenges and are willing to share their experiences.

GOD USES BROKEN THINGS BEAUTIFULLY;

BROKEN CLOUDS POUR RAIN,

BROKEN SOIL SETS AS FIELDS,

BROKEN CROPS YIELD SEEDS,

BROKEN SEEDS GIVE LIFE TO NEW PLANTS.

SO, WHEN YOU FEEL YOU ARE BROKEN,

BE REST ASSURED THAT GOD IS PLANNING TO

UTILIZE YOU FOR SOMETHING GREAT.

~ANONYMOUS

Biography

FREDA STEVENSON

Freda is a resident of Cedar Hill, Tennessee. She graduated from Jo Byrns High School. She is a Tennessee State University college graduate with a Bachelor of Science in Health Information Management. Freda is a senior Clinical Research Data Specialist in Oncology Research at Vanderbilt University Medical Center. She has been working in oncology research since October 1, 2000. Before being employed at Vanderbilt University Medical Center, she worked in several roles for the Metropolitan Nashville General Hospital (Meharry) for over twenty-six years.

Freda is the mother of one son (Stephen Alexander "Chris Zander"). She is passionate about caring for others and helping them see their value and fullest potential in society. Freda has a kind, genuine spirit and a heart of gold.

She enjoys putting a smile on the faces of those around her. Her hobbies include interior decorating, nature walks, bird watching, flower gardening, sewing, and uplifting and motivating others who struggle with self-approval and esteem regarding social acceptance, weight, and life issues.

Finding Love and
Peace Within.

PURPOSE
JACQUELINE WOODARD

DEDICATED TO:

Angelica McKissick

Nataleigh Drew

Fallyne Davis

Cayden McKissick

Jacquie Woodard

PURPOSE

Becoming who God created me to BE

I have had to learn to be patient with myself,

Healing takes time.

Healing requires a different level of kindness and forgiveness.

Healing means changes are coming.

Becoming is not easy.

Be patient with the healing process.

God is strengthening your heart while you are sitting alone in the garden.

Special types of flowers are meant to bloom later.

I am a late bloomer.

While the dew is still on the roses, before my thoughts are all over the place, I love to reflect on my relationship with God. Oftentimes, we use that so loosely, but I encourage everyone that reads the inscribed words to truly carve out the time to enrich their relationship with God. If you do not have a one-on-one relationship, I encourage you to develop that daily connection by carving out the time in the early morning. As women, we carry so much that weighs us down. We find ourselves heavily burdened with family issues, financial issues, and, of course, work issues that it seems there is no time for self-care and a personal relationship with God.

My Sister in Christ, how many times have you been called by another name other than the name God called you at birth? If we all think back from childhood to the present day, our name has changed several times. My God-given name is Jacqueline, derived from the French culture. Inherent meaning: Substitute, Spiritual Connotation: Renewal Scripture Job 33:4 KJV *"The Spirit of God has made me, and the breath of the Almighty gives me life."* Yvonne is Hebrew, meaning Gift or Grace of God, Yew wood, or Archer. I am all the meanings of my name; I know whose I am and that my life reflects who God created me to be. Am I frightened to live the life that God created in me? Yes, I am questioning my life at this age and season, and I still cry and seek God more daily.

Over the course of my life, I have walked on eggshells to prevent hurting people's feelings or bringing them embarrassment because they didn't understand the God-given energy instilled in me, but that time has come and gone. Now, I am walking in purpose to the fullest, and if my outward boldness frightens anyone, I do not apologize or walk with my head down. God has pruned me to be a trailblazer and generational curse-breaker.

Little girl, little girl… the little girl inside of me that grew up at 1023 Childress Street still seeks the validation that she never received from those that were supposed to encourage, nourish and promote her dreams. I ask God to heal the broken pieces and places inside my heart, mind, and soul so that I can grow and love His people with that special love that He wished for us here on earth. In the summer of 2008, I was ordained as a Minister of the Gospel to teach the Word of God. I have fallen short of doing that, fearing what people will say, but not anymore.

Teenager, teenager… you are still seeking your identification/identity in this big world. My formative years propelled me into the next chapter(s) of life. As I began this journey, it was crucial to have that one relationship that would be constant and loving. I contribute my introduction to my Christian faith to my grandmother, Cora B. Woodard, whom I would walk with to church on Sunday mornings and some Wednesday nights for Bible study, learning to study God's word and developing the understanding of life through the creator of all things.

Young woman, young woman… you have now graduated from high school to the next phase of your life. Where do you go from here? The options are numerous, and the path is wide open. So, where did you go from here? Oftentimes, when I thought of my future, a wedding and children entered the picture, a vision board with just thoughts drawn on a piece of paper. What were my options after earning an associate degree in my early twenties? One was to continue nurturing my relationship and seek my place with God, which was incredibly important to me. As I matured, I earned a bachelor's and master's degree to enhance my ability to support myself financially.

My favorite scripture has always been Philippians 4:13, "*I can do all things through Christ who strengthens me.*" My daily prayer as a young woman was:

Our Father, which art in heaven, I come to you asking that you help me to accomplish everything that you have for me to do to help me to fulfill my purpose. I want to please You as I owe it all to You. Please lead Jacqueline where she is needed as I grow in my walk with You. In Jesus' name, Amen.

As my purpose has become clearer, I reflect on the scripture of Jeremiah 29:11, which reminds me that God has a plan for my life, a plan to prosper me and not to harm me. I thank God daily for knowing His voice and hearing

Him clearly as it pertains to the direction for the next chapters in my life.

At the age of twenty-eight, I got married on October 30, 1988, on a beautiful Sunday afternoon. The ceremony was simple but elegant. I wore a beautiful baby blue gown hand sewn and designed by my sister Angela; she did a beautiful job. The gown was adorned in white pearls with a matching headpiece. I still have these items today, not because of the wedding itself, but because there is a sentimental value that I can't replace.

I had been married for ten years when the life I had built fell apart in December 1999. While going through the separation and divorce, I asked God for patience. I was led to this scripture, James 1:4, "*Let patience have her perfect work*." I wanted patience, and I wanted it right then at that moment. I realized God was patient with me; every time I cried, I considered that to be a time that God was teaching me His good and perfect will.

The divorce taught me many things, primarily that I needed God more than ever. I am happy that He is our friend as we go through and when we come out on the other side. He has never left or forgotten about us. The trials and tribulations are just a test of our ability to walk by faith and not by sight. I entered each day with prayer and a heart of thanksgiving because I almost lost my mind. I played the scenario over and over in my mind and heart. I remember just like it was yesterday as I am writing, and I am thankful that God granted me the desires of my heart.

The month was December 1999, and the words, the place, and the time are etched in my soul forever. I allowed that dark, ugly period to take up residence in my life long enough that I would not go to work because I was afraid of what people might say or think. As a mother of two precious babies, I had to protect them from the ugly behaviors that had entered our home, going in and out at all times of the night. A person that I did not know had entered my life. The lies, one after the other, began to take a toll on my mental and physical health.

It was fourteen months of the most delusional time of my life, staying at home day end and day out with the curtains drawn tight, never leaving for anything but to take my girls to school and pick them up. I protected my girls from everything that was our new norm from December until May, when school would be out for the summer. I thank God for giving me patience through the transition. I got relief on the last day of school. I packed the girls' clothes for the entire summer and took them to visit family. The next day I rented a U-Haul to move from the place and the person causing me pain. At this point, I had finally found my prayer closet and used it often. I felt much like David dancing before the Lord; my prayer was a plea for release and blessings.

Summer vacation finally ended. It was time for the girls to return home and enter the new school year, excited and ready to learn again. The girls had no idea that we would be living in our new place when they returned. There was excitement on their faces and many questions about who lived there. I told them we do, and they said no, we live down there. We went back and forth until I convinced them to come look inside. The new place was just what we needed! A few days before school started, we took a much-needed break and got in some summertime vacation as a new family.

I believe in my heart that I received the release my soul desired, but my heart refused to accept it as I began making the moves I needed. Once I let go, I came to grips with the outcome of what had to happen, and that was for me to heal and move into the next phase of my life. I began to smile and enjoy life as a single parent of two.

The greatest gift of the marriage was the birth of my daughter. Seeing her work daily in her God-given talent and raising my granddaughter is a joy and delight. I sit back and thank God for their lives as I pray over my daughter and granddaughter daily. I pray that they are blessed with every dream but, most of all, that they are a blessing to help the kingdom of God.

My first blessing is my oldest daughter, who I am exceedingly proud of. She is currently the managing director at the local hospital. The mother of a son, she is a football mom, a baseball mom, and a soccer mom. You can find her making jewelry pieces in her spare time or creating baked goods or candied apples in the kitchen.

The Power of a Smile

Mark 10:13-16

"A merry heart makes a cheerful countenance."

Proverbs 15:13

In my relationship with people, some things are so simple that they may be overlooked. For instance, a smile is the finest medium of exchange we have. A smile can dramatically change our appearance for the better. Once I realized that there was more to be thankful for beyond the trials and tribulations of heartbreak, I began to celebrate finding that inner peace with God, leading the way to a full recovery. The greatest relationship that we can birth is that one with God.

I encourage everyone to start the day with meditation and prayer, especially if you wish to feel uplifted and gain a newfound strength. As I approached the end of those dark days, I began to get comfortable in the mirror, looking up and smiling, saying these words:

"I am the head and not the tail. I am above and not beneath. I am blessed going in and blessed coming out."

I had to begin walking in the promise of the scripture Deuteronomy 28:13. As I continued to get comfortable with my new single life, I began to mingle with people again, returning to the joyful woman that once never met a stranger. I returned to looking up and smiling, knowing that God had not left me even in what I considered my darkest days and nights. I thank God for returning my joyous spirit and using it to help heal other women on this same journey. I am an ordained Minister and Elder, and God uses me to speak life into women. Every opportunity I have to speak life into someone, I say yes. Recently, I received my certification as a Master Life Coach.

You know doors are opening when complete strangers open the door and say I saw this, that, or the other, and I want you to join me as we present this new idea. God keeps His promises daily.   Sisters hold tight to the promises of God, which are Yes, and Amen. He is a restorer of all things Good and Great.

Sincerely,

Jacqueline

SELF CARE
JOURNAL

"For I know the plans that I think toward you, says the Lord, thoughts of peace and not of evil,

to give you a hope and a future."

Jeremiah 29:11

The journal is a gift from me to you, the owner of this great Anthology. I encourage you to read the scripture references or those you choose to meditate on and write your thoughts and revelations on the enclosed pages.

5-minute journaling
Date:

"For we are God's handiwork, created in Christ Jesus to do good works, which God prepared in advance for us to do."
Ephesians 2:10

5-minute journaling
Date:

"For God has not given us a spirit of fear and timidity but of power, love, and self-discipline."
 2 Timothy 1:7

5-minute journaling   Date:

"Better to be patient than powerful; better to have self-control than to conquer a city." Proverbs 16:32

5-minute journaling Date:

"Don't worry about anything; instead, pray about everything. Tell God what you need and thank him for all he has done. Then you will experience God's peace, which exceeds anything we can understand. His peace will guard our hearts and mind as we live in Christ Jesus."
Philippians 4:6-7

5-minute journaling Date:

"For who can know the Lord's thoughts? Who knows enough to give him advice? And who has given him so much that He needs to pay it back? For everything comes from Him and exists by His power and is intended for His glory to Him forever." Romans 11:34-36

5-minute journaling   Date:

"I pray that your love will overflow more and more, and that you will keep on growing in knowledge and understanding." Philippians 1:9-10

5-minute journaling Date:

"Finally, be strong in the Lord and in the strength of his might. Put on the whole armor of God, that you might be able to stand against the wiles of the devil." Ephesians 6: 10-11

5-minute journaling   Date:

"Little children, you are of God, and have overcome them; for he who is in you is greater than he who is in the world."
1 John 4:4

5-minute journaling   Date:

"My sacrifice, O God, is a broken spirit; a broken and contrite heart you, God, will not despise." Psalm 51:17

BIO

JACQUELINE WOODARD

Jacqueline Y. Woodard holds an Associate Degree in Banking, BS in Human Resource Management, and an MBA in Business Administration. Jacqueline has also received her Certification as a Certified Master Life Coach through Transformation Academy.

In February 2017, Jacqueline launched All In The Family Comprehensive Enrichment Center, which holistically works to undergird every member of the family to increase the many facets of life through exposure to their personal needs. The company was successfully vetted by the Small Business Administration in 2018 and 2019.

Jacqueline has over thirty (30) plus years of business experience. In those years, she was the Executive Director of several community service programs that exposed her to the needs of her community. Under the umbrella of All In The Family Comprehensive Enrichment Center, the community has access to opportunities to investigate their entrepreneurial spirit through "Dare 2 Dream" The Business Academy. The future will be bright for hundreds of children when the plans for Young Academic Achievers Early Learning Center are complete. It is currently in the developmental stages. The Learning Center will focus on electronic learning in early childhood education.

As a Certified Mentor for Score of Nashville, this volunteer opportunity allows Jacqueline to meet the needs of Small Business owners at start-up and follow the business through the many facets of becoming an entrepreneur. All In The Family has been a past host of the Small Business

Administration "**InnovateHer**" seeking Small Businesses that can change the lives of Americans with their innovative and unique products or services.

Jacqueline's early years of her professional career started with Meharry Medical College, where her knowledge and understanding of the Federal Office of Management and Budgeting was an asset. Jacqueline was responsible for the day-to-day operation of over $8 million dollars in grants and contracts for the Research and Development Programs. Jacqueline moved through the ranks from financial analyst in the Grants and Contracts Office to the Assistant Director of the Area Health Education Center.

Jacqueline has an array of experiences, but her love for grant writing and research drives her passion to assist other organizations to reach the potential of growth and expansion that best fits the Mission and Motto of the organization.

Jacqueline wrote and directed an Adult Education program at YWCA in Memphis, TN. Under this adult program, participants received educational training to prepare each adult to sit for their General Education Diploma, Warehouse/Logistics, Computer operations, Customer service, Carpentry, and construction. The program ran successfully until funding was lost at the end of the budget period. The program also included a job training and certification component working with this same age range of youth to acquire skilled training accreditation.

Executive Director for the Workforce Investment Opportunity Act, this program was a continuation program of the Robertson County Board of Education. Under this program, adults receive educational training and testing to receive a General Education Degree.

Bransford Youth Community Development Center, a budding community program for elementary-age children, provided before and after school programs for K through 5 in the age range. The building where the program was housed was condemned, and the program was closed due to a lack of meeting space to host the program.

The program received funding from various sources that included several community organizations, such as the local police and fire department.

Finding Love and
Peace Within.

Printed in July 2023
by Rotomail Italia S.p.A., Vignate (MI) - Italy